Safety Tips

real kids/real science books contain lots of ideas and
suggestions for observing and collecting animals and plants in
woods, fields, ponds, drainage ditches, and at the shore.
If you follow a few simple rules, your adventures will be safe
and enjoyable.

▶ Plan your field trips with your parents or guardian, even if you
  are going to collect or observe in a familiar place. Make sure
  they are aware if you need to venture into even shallow water.
▶ Wear appropriate dress. Protect your feet when wading;
  protect your arms and legs in heavy underbrush.
▶ Share your adventures with a friend.

Ornithology

"Study nature, not books." —LOUIS AGASSIZ

Ornithology

written by Ellen Doris
original photography by Len Rubenstein

PRODUCED IN ASSOCIATION WITH
The Children's School of Science
Woods Hole, Massachusetts

 THAMES AND HUDSON

What is this book about?

This is not only a book about birds. This is a book about Ornithology, which is the study of birds, their evolution, and their place in the environment today. You will find lots of projects, field trips, ideas, and suggestions to help you study the birds in your area.

How to use this book

Ornithology is organized as a collection of separate experiments, investigations, and discoveries. It shows you where to look for different kinds of birds, and how to study them in relation to their natural habitats. You don't have to follow the book step-by-step from beginning to end. We suggest you browse through it first. Look for a field trip that's easy to do near your home, like nest watching—even city parks are home to many kinds of birds. This book will be a lot more fun if you share some of the projects and field trips with someone else, a friend or parent. And always remember to be a safe scientist—plan your trips with an adult.

Where can you get equipment and field guides?

Except for a pair of binoculars (which you can borrow), you shouldn't need much equipment to explore the world of birds. If you want to go farther, there is a list on page 62 of equipment and field guides that you can order from biological supply houses. But don't feel you have to order all of them at once. Some of the equipment, like the nest-viewer on page 40, is fairly simple to build yourself.

What is a brood parasite? And how do you pronounce Sphenisciformes?

Check out the glossary on page 63, which defines all the terms that are printed in **bold** type. But don't get bogged down trying to pronounce long Latin names; sound them out as well as you can and go on.

Think for yourself

You'll probably have to adapt some of the projects you find in this book. Remember, not every project or field trip goes according to plan. For instance, birds may not come to eat at your feeder. Have you put out the right sort of food for the birds in your area? Is there too much noise or movement nearby? Think about what may have gone wrong, and try again.

The Children's School of Science Woods Hole, Massachusetts

Each summer, in an old-fashioned schoolhouse whose rooms are crowded with plants, nets, microscopes, and bubbling aquaria, several hundred children between the ages of seven and sixteen attend classes for two hours each morning. Led by teachers who are experts in their field, the children take frequent field trips and work with each other on projects and experiments. The classes are informal, and courses range from Seashore Exploration to Ornithology to Neurobiology. For over seventy-five years, this remarkable institution has fostered the joy of discovery by encouraging direct observation of natural phenomena.

Contents

This book is dedicated to the teachers and students of the Children's School of Science, without whose enthusiastic help it would not have been possible.

Copyright © 1994 Thames and Hudson Inc., New York
First published in the United States in 1994 by Thames and Hudson Inc.,
500 Fifth Avenue, New York, New York 10110

Photos copyright © Len Rubenstein unless otherwise indicated.

Library of Congress Catalog Card Number 93-61888

Designed, typesetting, and pre-press production by Beth Tondreau Design ■ Managing Editor, Laurance Rosenzweig

Color separations made by The Sarabande Press ■ Printed and bound in Hong Kong

Introduction

You can find birds just about everywhere. Some dive after fish in the chilly waters of the Antarctic Ocean, while others hunt snakes and lizards in the desert. Some build their nests behind waterfalls, others prefer caves, and still others raise families on top of tall city buildings. Your own neighborhood is a good place to start learning about birds and **ornithology**, which is the study of birds.

What makes a bird?

At least 8,700 different kinds, or **species**, of birds live on this planet! This large, diverse group of animals includes hummingbirds so small people sometimes mistake them for insects, and ostriches that stand taller than a person. It includes thrushes and sandpipers that blend in with their surroundings, and peacocks and parrots whose bright colors stand out.

Despite their many differences, however, all birds share some basic characteristics. Some are easy to see, while others are **internal**, or on the inside.

All birds have...

- **Feathers.** Birds are the only animals that have feathers.

- **Two legs.** Birds use their legs and feet for standing and walking. Birds may also use their legs to swim, perch, carry things, or dig.
- **Two wings.** Most birds use their wings to fly. Even birds that can't fly, like penguins and kiwis, have wings.

- **Bills or beaks.** These special mouthparts can pick up food and break or tear it into pieces. Birds don't have teeth in their beaks, as we do in our jaws, and they do not chew their food.

- **Eggs.** All birds hatch from eggs. A bird egg has a hard outer **shell** that protects the developing chick within, and keeps it from drying out.

With its wing spread open, you can see the different kinds of feathers this blue jay uses to fly. (See Feathers, p. 31.)

- **Warm blood.** Birds are **homeothermic**, or "warm blooded." This means they can maintain a body temperature that is quite constant, and different from the surrounding air. Birds also have specialized skeletons, and efficient hearts and lungs.

Ways to learn about birds

There are many ways to study birds. You can learn to identify dozens of species in the field, or focus on the behavior of one familiar bird. You might listen to bird songs, observe nests, or learn all you can about a particular family of birds. This book will show you some different ways to find out about birds. Try them out, and see which aspects of ornithology most interest you.

Classification

Scientists group all of the animals in the world together in one large **kingdom**, the *Animalia*. This kingdom is made up of many smaller groups. One is the **class** *Aves*, or birds. Ornithologists recognize nearly nine thousand different species of birds. They classify these species into various **orders** and **families**. Learning about avian orders and families can help you identify a new bird you see, for the birds within a group usually share important physical characteristics that you will start to recognize. It can also help you think about how different species may have evolved, for scientists group together the species they believe are most closely related. This system of classifying species is called **taxonomy**.

Orders and families

Scientists divide the class *Aves* into about twenty-nine orders (some use fewer). Each order is further divided into families, and each family contains a number of **genera** (plural for **genus**). Finally, each genus contains a number of closely related species. For the most part, birds will only mate with members of their own species. It will take time to learn the characteristics of all twenty-nine orders, and to know which families, genera, and species belong to each!

Begin by learning about a few orders that include some birds you often see. Two orders of birds are described here, together with some of the families they include. As you read about them, think if you have ever seen a bird that fits each description.

The *Anseriformes* are the swans, ducks, geese, and screamers. Most are aquatic. Their young are **precocial**, which means they are covered with down when they hatch, and are soon able to walk and look for food. The screamers (in the family *Anhimidae*) have feet that are only slightly webbed, but the ducks, geese, and swans (*Anatidae*) have a full web connecting their three front toes. Members of the family *Anatidae* have long necks, and long, flat bills.

The *Passeriformes*, or perching birds, are adapted for perching in trees. They have three toes facing forward, and one highly developed back toe, all at the same level. Young perching birds are **altricial**, that is, they are undeveloped when they hatch and must be fed and kept warm by their parents for a period of time. The *Passeriformes* include over five thousand species, more than any other order. The songbirds familiar to many people are included in this group. Wrens (*Troglodytidae*), warblers (*Parulidae*), and crows, magpies, and jays (*Corvidae*) are just a few of the many families in this order.

Ducks and swans both belong to the family Anatidae, *and share the family traits of broad bills, webbed feet, and aquatic habitats.*

Naming birds

Most people refer to birds by common names, such as "robin," "redstart," and "roadrunner." Some species have more than one common name. For example, the osprey is also known as a fish hawk, and the bird called a "shag" in parts of Canada and Maine is known as a "cormorant" further south. To further complicate matters, some common names refer to more than one kind of bird. The term "seagull," for instance, can mean any of the large, white birds familiar to beach–goers; yet scientists recognize over forty separate species of gulls! To avoid confusion, ornithologists use a two–part Latin name to label each kind of bird. The first part of the name is shared with all of the related species that make up a genus, and the second part is given to just one species. Thus, *Larus argentatus* is the herring gull, and *Larus delawarensis* is the ring–billed gull. Both common and scientific names will be used in this book.

Bird classifications are continually being revised to reflect new

Evolutionary cousins: the herring gull (top) and the ring-billed gull (bottom).

discoveries and understanding. Even the concept of "species" changes over time, as ornithologists learn more about birds. A single species may be reclassified as a group of related species, or the other way around.

This blue jay is a smaller and more colorful member of the same family that includes the crows, Corvidae.

Taxonomy

KINGDOM: **Animalia (the animals)**
PHYLUM: **Chordata (the chordates, or animals that have a dorsal nerve chord, gills, and a notochord during some stage of their development)**
CLASS: **Aves (the birds)**
ORDER: **Anseriformes (swans, ducks, geese, and screamers)**
FAMILY: **Anatidae (waterfowl: swans, geese, and ducks; waterbirds with webbed feet and broad, flattened bills)**
SUBFAMILY: **Anserinae (swans, whistling ducks, and geese)**
GENUS: **Cygnus**
SPECIES: **Cygnus olor (mute swan)**

More Orders

Struthioniformes—ostriches
Sphenisciformes—penguins
Pelicaniformes—pelicans, cormorants, gannets, anhingas
Falconiformes—vultures, hawks, falcons
Galliformes—pheasants, chickens, game birds
Ciconiiformes—herons, bitterns, storks, ibises
Gruiformes—cranes
Charadriiformes—shorebirds, gulls, alcids
Columbiformes—pigeons and doves.
Psittaciformes—parrots, lorries, cockatoos
Strigiformes—owls
Apodiformes—swifts and hummingbirds

GETTING STARTED

Begin your study of birds by finding some birds to watch. They don't need to be any special kind; in fact, you don't even need to know what kind they are! If you watch them closely for a while, you will discover many things about how they look and what they do.

Birds sometimes nest in ivy on walls.

Where to go, what to bring

Birds live just about everywhere. You can find them in city parks, suburban back yards, vacant lots, and parking lots. Make your first field trip to a part of your neighborhood where you remember seeing birds, or where you think birds would be likely to live. You don't need to bring any special equipment with you. Your first trip can be a time to discover where birds can be found in your neighborhood, and to see how many you can spot. Plan to wear comfortable clothing that suits the weather and the area where you will walk. Wear long pants if you plan to go through tall weeds or brush, especially if ticks are common where you live. Tuck your pant legs into your socks for added protection from ticks.

Birds at a distance

Many of the birds you see will be far away, or will fly off when they first notice you. Watch them anyway. Even if you aren't able to get a good look at the color of their feathers, or see them for long, you can still notice many important things. Try to describe the way they fly through the air, and listen for their songs.

Some birds can soar through the air, rarely moving their wings. Others hover, or fly with deep, steady wing beats, or flap and then glide.

If the bird you have spotted takes off, try to follow it with your eyes until it lands. Walk slowly and quietly towards its new perch to get another look at it.

Birds up close

Some birds, like pigeons and herring gulls, are used to living among people, and you will be able to watch them at close range. Take a good look at the colors of their feathers, and the way they walk and use their wings. You can often get close to shyer birds as well. Just walk to a place where you will be comfortable sitting or standing for a few minutes, then stay as still and quiet as you can. Birds that were alarmed when you first approached will often come out of hiding once you stop moving around, and will walk or fly quite near you.

Binoculars

Although binoculars are not absolutely necessary for birdwatching, many people like to use them because they can give a close-up view of birds that are far away. If you do not already own binoculars but are thinking about getting a pair, try out a friend's to see what using them is like. There are many different binoculars on the market, so talk to experienced birdwatchers to find out what type they find easiest to use. Most birdwatchers use binoculars that have a wide field of view, and are able to magnify an image about seven or eight times. Binoculars with a central focusing knob are easiest to use. Some birdwatchers also use special telescopes called spotting scopes to look at birds (See page 62 for information on ordering binoculars.)

Think about timing

Try looking for birds at different times of the day. Some birds start singing before dawn, while others hunt at night. Many birds are most active early in the morning. If you have trouble finding birds in your neighborhood, schedule a bird walk at sunrise.

You may find you can get a closer look at small birds that are hidden among tree branches if you make a sharp "pssh-pssh-pssh" sound. Some birds will hop out to the ends of branches and look around when they hear this sound.

Neighborhood Birds

Above, a flock of pigeons looks for food on the sidewalk. Below, three pigeons sun themselves on a roof.

nce you have found a good birdwatching place in your neighborhood, try to get familiar with one or two of the species you see there. Choose kinds that are easy to recognize, and fun to watch. Once you have decided which birds to study, observe them as often as you can, and take note of all the places where you see them. Your observations will help you to figure out what they eat, what times of day they are most active, and where they nest.

Pigeons

The pigeon, *Columba livia*, was originally an Old World bird. Some were caught and **domesticated**, or raised by people. People used pigeons as food, and homing pigeons were used to carry messages. Over time, pigeons were brought to many other parts of the world. Inevitably, some of these domestic birds escaped and established themselves in the wild. Look for them on buildings and city sidewalks, in parks, and around farms. Where you find one pigeon you will usually find many, for they are highly **social** birds. Pigeons often feed in large flocks, and **roost** (perch and rest) together at night. Many nest in groups, as well.

Most pigeons are a grayish blue color with pale gray wings and shiny, iridescent necks. However, you will also find white and brown pigeons. These differences in color and pattern can help you recognize individual birds within a group, and keep track of what they do. Pigeons are particularly good birds to study because they are so used to living among people that you can often get quite close to them. You will be able to observe them without binoculars for long periods of time.

Keep a lookout for nests as well as adult birds. Pigeons originally nested on cliff ledges and in caves, but now you are more apt to find their nests on window ledges, under railroad trestles, in barns, and in other nooks and crannies built by people. In warm parts of the country, many pigeons begin nesting in winter. In colder climates, look for males carrying small twigs to their nests in late winter and early spring. A female pigeon usually just lays one or two eggs in her nest, but once her chicks have left the nest, she may rear another one or two broods.

House sparrows

The house sparrow, *Passer domesticus*, was deliberately introduced to the United States in the 1850s. It is now common in cities, towns, and suburbs throughout much of North America. In the spring and summer you can recognize male house sparrows by their gray heads, black bibs, and short, stubby dark beaks. During the fall and winter, the brownish tips of their new feathers may partly cover the bib, and their dark beaks turn yellow. Females and young birds have a light stripe behind their eyes, and dingy white breasts. House sparrows eat seeds and insects, and you will also find them feeding on crumbs.

Like pigeons, house sparrows are used to living among people, and you will be able to observe them at close range. Look for their nests—large, round collections of grasses and other material—in any kind of cavity, nook, or cranny. House sparrows nest on buildings, in signs, and in tree cavities and birdhouses. They are so common that they may claim many of the natural cavities in an area for nest sites, leaving few for other cavity-nesting species, such as the eastern bluebird.

House sparrows gather in groups to roost during fall and winter evenings. Dozens of them may take cover in the ivy growing on a building, a hedge, or some other sheltered place. Unlike most other birds, they will also use their nests for shelter during the winter.

House sparrows will nest in all sorts of cavities. If you want to attract them, think about putting up a birdhouse like this one.

House sparrows are also called English sparrows, although they are not closely related to native North American sparrows. They belong to a family of birds called the weaver finches, who typically weave plant fibers together into a spherical nest that opens on the side.

13

Identifying Birds

I t's fun to watch birds, whether you know what to call them or not. Often, though, you will want to identify the birds you see. Wild birds can be tricky to identify. They are often on the move, so it can be hard to get a good, long look at them. Luckily, many birds have shapes, color patterns, and ways of behaving that you can learn to recognize at a glance.

When you spot a bird

When you first notice a bird, watch to see how it looks, and what it is doing. You may want to focus on it with your binoculars for a better view. Describe it to a friend, or just to yourself. Note the color, shape, and size of various parts, as well as your general impressions.. After the bird has flown away, or after you have studied it for a while, jot down your description in a notebook, and make a quick sketch of the bird. Your careful observations and notes will help you recognize the bird if you ever see another like it. You won't always get a good look at every aspect of a bird. For example, if the light is poor, a bird's colors may not show up. Don't worry; just describe whatever you *can* see. You will soon be able to recognize many species based on a few important aspects of their appearance.

Using a field guide

A field guide can help you identify the birds you see. Field guides to the birds contain pictures of different birds, and short descriptions about their habits. They point out **field marks**, or details of a bird's appearance that can help you identify it at a distance. Many guides also have **range maps** that show where each species usually lives.

After you have looked carefully at a bird and described it to yourself, you can see if any of the pictures in your field guide look similar. Compare your own description of the bird with the pictures in your guide that most closely match what you saw. Check the range maps to see if the birds listed in your guide live in the area where you have been birdwatching. Also read the text, and check the measurements and behaviors it describes against your own observations.

Identifying birds can be difficult. An individual may be a little larger, darker, or more brightly colored than the one pictured in your guide. Or you may see a bird that has wandered far from the place where it usually lives. You may have to make observations over time, or consult an experienced birdwatcher, in order to identify some of the birds you see.

Jot down descriptions and make sketches of the birds you see.

Other ways to identify birds

Even ornithologists find some birds difficult to identify! Certain warblers look so much alike that researchers can only tell them apart by looking at their nests, and some small flycatchers are most easily distinguished by their songs. In fact, some birds, like owls and whippoorwills, are often heard but seldom seen. You can buy a tape recording of bird songs, or check one out from your library.

One species or two? Or three?

When you first begin to study birds, it may be hard to tell if you are looking at two members of the same species, or two completely different birds. This is because many kinds of birds look a lot alike, even though they have different habits and never mate with one another. Sometimes members of a single species can confuse us, because their appearance may change with the seasons, or as they grow older. Further, the male members of a species may not have the same colors and markings as the females. Keep track of the different birds you see by sketching or photographing them, and writing short descriptions. Your notes will help you remember what you have seen, and make good use of field guides and other references.

You can see this catbird's black cap and gray body; it also has a patch of chestnut feathers on its back.

Field marks, like the red forehead of this male house finch, can help you identify a bird that is partly hidden.

Young robins, like this one, have speckled breasts. As they get older, their breasts turn dark red.

The crest on the head of this Northern cardinal is a striking feature and easy to spot, even in poor light.

Two members of the same species may look quite different. In the summertime, male goldfinches have bright yellow bodies, while females are olive-yelow. In the winter, both sexes are olive-yellow.

Birds have differrent shapes, or **silhouettes**, that can help you recognize them at a distance.

How Birds Are Built

irds have bodies that are like ours in some ways, but very different in others. Next time you are close to a bird, study the way its body is "put together." Think about the features all birds have in common, and how different species are adapted for life in particular kinds of places. Pet stores, zoos, and nature centers that keep some birds in cages are good places to study bird bodies. Caged birds can't fly far, so you will be able to get a good look at them.

Made to fly

Most birds are built to fly. They have streamlined bodies that move easily through the air, lightweight skeletons, and strong muscles to power their wings. Birds have backbones that are fused together (unlike ours, which allow our backs to bend and wiggle). This keeps a bird's body stiff as it moves through the air. Feathers provide lightweight insulation, as well as contribute to the streamlined body shape.

Birds have **tendons** that connect the bones of their lower legs and feet to muscles in the "thigh" and "drumstick," so they are able to move their lower legs and feet with-

out a lot of heavy muscle. Different species of birds have different kinds of feet. Some feet can get a good grip on prey, while others are good for swimming, wading, or perching.

Eyes and ears

Birds have well-developed eyes, and very keen eyesight. In this owl skull, the eye sockets seem to take up most of the skull! Birds' brains have a large **optic lobe** that processes information from the eyes.

Most birds have eyes on the sides of their heads. This allows them to see what is in front of them, and to each side, and some of what is behind them–all at once! Owls have both eyes facing front, as we do.

An owl's skull.

This gives owls good **depth perception**, that is, they can judge distances accurately. However, it limits their **field of vision**, or how far around they can see. Birds have eyelids, and they also have a transparent **nictating membrane** that can quickly move across the eye to moisten and clean it.

Birds have ears, one on each side of their heads. The ears don't show, because they are covered with a layer of feathers and birds don't have **external ears** that stick out from the body. Birds have a highly developed sense of hearing.

All birds have a beak or bill. Bills come in many shapes and sizes. Herons have long, sturdy bills that enable them to grab fish and frogs out of the water, while sparrows have short bills that can pick up insects and crack open seeds. A hummingbird's bill can reach deep into flowers and suck out nectar, while a woodpecker can peck into tree bark. Shorebirds have sensitive beaks that can feel for prey in the sand.

A bird has two nostrils in its beak that connect to air passages that lead to lungs.

All mammals, including people, have seven small neck bones called **vertebrae**. Different species of birds, however, have different numbers of neck bones. Herons have 16 or 17, and swans have up to 25!

| NICTATING MEMBRANE | SMALL EARHOLE | BEAK AND TONGUE | NOSTRILS | MANY VERTEBRAE |

Reconstructing a chicken wing

One way to learn more about a bird's body is to study the skin, muscles, and bones of a chicken from the grocery store. Buy a whole chicken, instead of one that is already cut into pieces, so that you can see how the wings and legs attach to the body, and how they bend. You will see pores on the skin where feathers once grew. These form lines, called feather tracts. You can also see that the chicken's breast, or "white meat," contains large, powerful muscles that move the wings.

Directions:

1. After you have looked over the whole chicken, get help to cut one wing off.
2. Cook the wing in a pot of water until the skin and meat become soft.
3. Remove the wing and let it cool. (You can save the broth in the pot to make soup with if you want.)
4. Pull as much of the skin and bone off the wing as you can. Then return the bones to the pot and cook them a while longer.
5. Remove the bones from the pot and cool them.
6. Use an old toothbrush to scrub off any remaining bits of muscle.
7. Study the different bones, then reassemble them on a piece of cardboard. You can use white glue to fix them in place.
8. If you wish, you can label the bones.

The bones in a bird's wing are similar to the bones in our arms. The thickest bone in the chicken's wing is called the **humerus**. The part of a bird's wing that contains the humerus is the part that joins the bird's body. (Your own humerus is in your upper arm, and stretches from your shoulder to your elbow.) The **radius** and **ulna** are the two slender bones that attach to the humerus. (These bones are in your

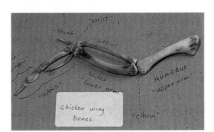

lower arm, between your elbow and wrist.) Because there are two bones in our lower arm, we can rotate this part of our body. Birds are able to rotate the middle section of their wings, too. The small bones in the "end" part of a bird's wing are similar to the bones in our wrist and hand.

Next time you see a bird in flight, think about what the bones inside its wings are like, and how they allow the wings to move.

AT A MARSH

Salt water marshes are good places to look for long-legged wading birds, like herons and egrets. At low tide you may be able to walk far into the marsh, or wade up shallow tidal creeks to look for birds. Keep track of the time so you will be back on "high ground" before the tide rolls in again. Bring along a pair of binoculars, and wear old sneakers, boots, or water shoes to protect your feet.

Great Blue Heron

The snowy egret (Egretta thula) breeds from northern California, Oklahoma, and Maine through South America. Groups of snowy egrets can be found in particular parts of some other states. Their pure, white feathers often stand out against the marsh grass.

Snowy egrets

You can recognize the snowy egret (*Egretta thula*) by its thin, black bill with yellow skin at the base. Adult snowy egrets have black legs with bright yellow feet, or "golden slippers," while immature birds have duller feet. You can check for the yellow feet when an egret takes to the air, for it will fly with its long legs trailing behind it, and its neck pulled back in a tight "S" curve.

Snowy egrets eat small crabs, shrimp, minnows, and other small marsh animals. You will sometimes see a snowy egret wade into shallow water or simply stand on the bank to look for food. Or you may see one tramp about in the shallows and stir up food with its shuffling feet. You may not be able to see just what the egrets you observe are catching, but you can find out what kind of food is available by sifting through the surface mud, and drawing a net through the shallow marsh water.

These days, snowy egrets are extending their breeding range along the northeast coast of the United States. In the early 1900s, however, they were quite rare. Hunters killed snowy egrets along with many other species during the 19th and early 20th centuries, and sold their feathers to decorate hats and other articles of clothing. Fortunately, laws were passed that prohibited the hunting of most kinds of birds, and snowy egrets are now common again in many places.

Green herons

Green herons, *Butorides striatus*, are common in developed areas as well as remote wetlands throughout the eastern United States, the midwest, and in parts of the southwest and west coast. When the weather turns cold, they leave the northern parts of their range and fly south.

You will often spot a green heron fishing in a salt marsh, not far from a hunting egret. It may stand motionless and watch for prey, or stalk with slow, jerky steps. When it spots food, its bill darts out with surprising speed. Green herons eat frogs, fish, and other small aquatic animals. Like other herons, they have large, slightly webbed feet that allow them to walk in wet places without sinking into the mud.

Colonial life

Snowy egrets, green herons, and great blue herons usually nest in trees and shrubs. Their nests are large, flat platforms made of sticks and twigs. Often, many birds will nest near one another in a colony or heronry. Some heronries are small, while others contain hundreds or even thousands of nests!

Taxonomy

ORDER: *Ciconiiformes (wading birds with long legs, bills, and necks)*

FAMILY: *Ardeidae (herons, bitterns, and egrets— birds with long, straight bills, that fly with their heads drawn back)*

GENUS AND SPECIES: *Egretta thula, (Snowy egret), Ardea herodias,(Great blue heron), Butorides virescens (Green heron, also called the little green heron and green-backed heron)*

Bird Behavior

It is both fun and fascinating to watch what birds do. Once you begin to notice the way birds behave, you'll find yourself wondering just how, and why, they do what they do. Studying bird behavior can help you discover more about the way birds live, and how they relate to one another and their environment.

Behavior

Scientists call a bird's actions, or the things that it does, its **behavior**. To begin your study of bird behavior, find some birds that are easy to watch, then pay close attention to what they do. Keep track of what you notice in a notebook. You will observe some actions–like flying and feeding–over and over. And the more you watch, the more you will learn about the way different species perform these actions. Some behaviors, like eating and drinking, help individual birds stay alive and healthy. Other behaviors are social; they are signals one bird sends to another.

Many birds seem to "look around" before leaving a nest or sheltered area, or while they are perching.

Robins feed on the ground. They often run across the grass, then stop and tilt their heads to search for insects or earthworms.

A male house sparrow will sometimes shudder his wings and call when he is near a female, or near his nest.

I know what it did, but what does that mean?

Behaviors are things we can observe. Their meaning, however, is not always obvious. You can learn about the meaning of behavior by watching what happens before, during, and after a bird does a particular thing. For example, you might notice that a chickadee always turns its head in various directions before flying out of its nest box, or that a Canada goose in the park hisses when you approach it. Once you know when a particular behavior occurs and what follows it, you can think about how the behavior seems to function, and what it might be "saying." The chickadee's head-turning could be a way of looking around for danger. If the coast is clear, it can fly off to search for food. The goose's hiss may be a warning it gives when another animal has come too close.

Canada geese will hiss at you if you get too close. This is their way of saying "back off."

Sometimes it is possible to check out your theories about a bird's behavior by making further observations. You can also read about research on bird behavior in magazines and books about birds.

One of the challenges animal behaviorists face is trying to understand what an animal's behavior means in terms of its own life, rather than in human terms. For instance, when we see a bird making endless trips with caterpillars to its nest, it is easy to imagine that bird as a loving and devoted parent. However, birds aren't people, and such interpretations may not help us fully understand birds. Ornithologists believe that birds are driven to do a great many things by **instinct**. That is, they are "programmed" to behave in certain ways. Birds are also capable of learning, though, and their behavior may change over time as a result of their experiences.

BIRDS ON THE BEACH

You will see birds whenever you go to the beach. Gulls cry overhead, and fight over food left by the waves or careless picnickers. Cormorants fly low over the water, or rest on rocks and pilings. Schedule beach trips at different times of the day and tidal cycle to see the greatest variety of birds. A notebook will help you keep track of what you see, and a hat or sunscreen will protect your skin.

Little brown beach birds

At first glance, many shorebirds look about the same—they are small, brown, and on the run. As you watch them, however, you will notice that some have longer necks and bills than others, and that some have dark bands or other markings that set them apart. You may see some birds that tend to feed in groups, and others that feed alone. These physical characteristics and behaviors will help you recognize the different families of shorebirds, and some individual species as well.

Two families you are likely to spot on the beach are the sandpipers (family *Scolopacidae*) and the plovers (family *Charadriidae*). Both eat small

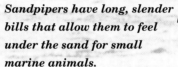

Sandpipers have long, slender bills that allow them to feel under the sand for small marine animals.

Semipalmated plovers breed from Alaska and the Canadian Arctic south to Nova Scotia and northern British Columbia.

marine animals. Sandpipers have long, slender legs and bills and rather long necks, while plovers have shorter bills and necks. The different bill length, leg length, and feeding style of each species allow it to collect food from particular places. For example, a long-legged bird can wade out into water where smaller birds cannot go. A long bill can probe for small animals buried down in the sand, while a shorter one may easily collect food at or near the surface.

Semipalmated plover

The black band below the neck of the semi-palmated plover will help you to recognize it during the spring and summer months. (Winter birds have a brown breastband.) At close range you can also see its beak, which is orange-yellow with a black tip. The term "semipalmated" refers to the plover's feet, which are only partly webbed. You can find the semipalmated plover (*Charadrius semipalmatus*) feeding on coastal beaches, tidal flats, salt marshes and along an inland lake shores. You may notice that they often run quickly along for a moment, then stop short and raise their heads. From time to time, they jab at the ground with their bills. This behavior is typical of many feeding plovers.

Taxonomy

ORDER: *Charadriiformes (a large, diverse group of wading or swimming birds that includes the shore birds, gulls, and alcids)*

FAMILIES:
Charadriidae (plovers, turnstones, and surfbirds), Scolopacidae (sandpipers), Haematopodidae (oystercatchers)

The American oystercatcher, Haematopus palliatus, is about the size of a chicken. It can stick its long, orange-red beak into an open mussel, clam, or oyster, and cut through its muscles before it can close its shell. Oystercatchers also eat barnacles and snails.

Beach Bird Food

Though it is easy to watch shorebirds feeding, it is often hard to see just what it is they collect with their bills. You can find out what food is available to them, though, by searching through the sand and shallow water. Look for beach bird food in areas where you have noticed birds feeding.

Equipment you will need:

- plastic shovel or garden trowel
- sieve or strainer
- plastic bucket

Directions:

1. Choose a part of the beach where you have seen birds feeding.
2. Look for marine animals around rocks, and in piles of seaweed. Save a sample of each kind of "food" in your bucket.
3. Look through shallow water to the sand below. You might find clues, such as lugworm castings or the siphon holes of clams, that tell you animals are buried there.
4. Dig up some sand or mud. You only need to dig as deep as a shorebird, so think about how long the beaks are on the birds you have seen.
5. Place the sand or mud in your sifter or strainer. Gently swirl it in shallow water to strain the sand out.
6. Once the sand and mud have been washed away, check to see what animals remain.

Look carefully in areas where you see shorebirds feeding to discover what they eat. Different species eat different prey.

CLAM SIPHON HOLE

Animals you might find in the sand:

- Clams

- Clam worms

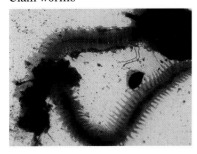

- Lugworms (casting)

- Trumpet worms

- Mole crabs

Animals you might find on rocks, or in piles of seaweed:

- Periwinkles

- Barnacles

- Mussels

An ancient food supply

For millions of years, horseshoe crabs have been laying their eggs along what is now the east coast of the United States. Pairs of crabs swim ashore beginning in May, and the females lay thousands of eggs in nests in the sand. The eggs are laid at high tide during the highest high tides, or **spring tides**. Over the days that follow, the tides will continue to ebb and flow, but the water will not rise as far up on the beach as it did during these spring tides. Instead of washing away, the horseshoe crab eggs are able to develop in the sandy nests. After a month they will hatch, and a new round of spring tides will wash them into the sea. That is, *some* of them will be washed to sea. Many eggs will never survive long enough to hatch. Instead, they will disappear into the bellies of gulls and shorebirds. Horseshoe crab eggs are an important source of food for shorebirds on their way north to breeding grounds in the Arctic.

Ornithologists can't always know for sure what birds have been eating simply by watching them. Sometimes, they dissect birds and examine the contents of their stomachs. Some birds vomit up **pellets** that contain undigestible parts of the things they have eaten. Scientists also study these pellets.

Young horseshoe crabs (above) and the shed "skin" of an adult horseshoe crab (left).

Terns

Terns are graceful fishing birds. Most have long, pointed bills and long, forked tails. Look for them as you walk along the coast. They often hover in the air, scanning the waves below for small fish and shrimp. Terns dive head-first into the water and catch prey with their beaks. Though they do have webbed feet, they don't do much swimming.

Common terns

There are forty–two species of terns world–wide. These are common terns, *Sterna hirundo*. In summer you can recognize them by their black cap and orange bills tipped with black. During the winter, the entire bill turns dark, and white feathers cover the forehead. On land, a tern's short legs seem out of proportion to its long, slender body.

Common terns nest on sandy beaches and rocky islands along the east coast of North America, and along inland waterways as well. Groups of terns nest together, forming **colonies**. Not much effort goes into nest building. Adult terns may pull a few bits of grass or sea-weed together, or just make a slight depression in the ground to hold their eggs. They put their energy into fishing for their hungry chicks, and protecting them from harm. If a person approaches a tern colony too closely, the adult birds will swoop around the intruder, shower-ing her with cries, droppings, and pecks on the head. This fierce be-havior has its drawbacks, however. While parents defend their nests from the air, their eggs and young are exposed to cold winds, hot sun, and hungry gulls.

Uncommon terns

In recent decades, many former tern colonies have been abandoned, or have failed to produce many young. Our activity is partly to blame; terns are easily disturbed when we build, drive vehicles, or play too close to their breeding grounds. The herring gull's success is another part of the problem. As herring gulls expand their range, they move onto islands and beaches already occupied by terns. In some cases the terns leave and look for nest sites elsewhere. In others they stay, but lose many eggs and chicks to the predatory gulls.

This young tern begs for food from one of its parents. It is already as large as an adult, but its white forehead shows it is still an immature bird. For a while longer, its parents will continue to bring it fish and protect it from predators.

Flying south

Common terns are **migratory** birds. They nest as far north as Labrador and Alberta in the summer, then take off for places as distant as Florida and South America. This seems like a spectacular feat for such delicate-looking birds. Unbelievably, it's a short haul compared to the journey some of

their close relatives undertake. Arctic terns (*Sterna paradisaea*) nest even further north than com-mon terns do, crossing the Arctic Circle to the Queen Elizabeth Islands and Greenland. When the breeding season is over, they fly across the Atlantic, then south along the west coasts of Europe and Africa to reach their winter feeding grounds in the Antarctic Ocean. For an individual nesting in the north-ernmost part of its range, one round trip can total 22,000 miles.

Taxonomy

ORDER: *Charadriiformes*
FAMILY: *Laridae*
  (gulls and terns)
SUBFAMILY: *Sterninae*
  (terns)
SOME SPECIES: *Sterna*
  hirundo (common tern),
  Sterna paradisaea
  (arctic tern)

AT THE DUMP

Your local dump or sanitary landfill can be a good place to watch birds. In coastal communities and near large lakes or reservoirs, gulls often flock to dumps in search of food. In a landfill near New York City, cattle egrets follow bulldozers just as they follow livestock in more rural areas. The bulldozers stir up flies that the egrets can eat, just as cattle flush insects from the grass. The dump can be an interesting place to study bird behavior—once you get used to the smell.

Born Scavengers

Herring gulls, *Larus argentatus*, are opportunistic feeders; they eat what is available. You can spot them scavenging for dead fish and shellfish along the shore; they scrounge for garbage in dumps in a similar fashion. Herring gulls eat worms and insects on playing fields and farmland, trail fishing boats to collect small fish and scraps that are thrown overboard, fly behind ferries to snatch snacks from passengers, and steal fish from terns and other gulls. They even eat the eggs and chicks of other birds, including neighboring herring gulls. You can recognize an adult herring gull by its snow white head and breast, gray back and wings, pinkish legs, and the red spot on its yellow bill.

Ring-billed and greater black-backed gulls are also opportunistic feeders, and you may find them alongside herring gulls at the dump or on the beach. The ring-billed gull, *Larus delawarensis*, is slightly smaller than the herring gull, with yellow legs and a black band around its yellow beak. The great black-backed gull, *Larus marinus*, is larger than the herring gull, and has much darker wings.

Goings-on amid garbage

Many of the gulls you see at the dump will be searching for food and eating. You may be surprised at the size of some of the things they are able to swallow! You will notice other behaviors, as well. Some gulls may "stand around" with their necks tucked in, and their wings close to their bodies. These birds are relatively relaxed. In an instant, though, one may stretch up its neck and look very alert. A gull assumes this posture when it is "sizing up" a situation to see whether or not danger threatens. Gulls make a variety of sounds. Sometimes one bird will cry out, and others will join in. These cries may help birds in the flock to stay in touch with one another. Other calls may sound a warning, "This is my place. Stay away!" A bird may call out and chase another away, or even steal food from another.

A major comeback

Although it is hard to believe, herring gulls and other gull species had become uncommon by the last quarter of the 19th century. Egg collecting and hunting had both taken their toll. But unlike some other species, herring gulls made a speedy recovery once it became illegal to shoot them. By the 1930s and '40s, "control" programs were being carried out along parts of the east coast to slow the herring gull's population explosion! Still, herring gulls seem to thrive alongside people. Though our development and use of the coast threatens many seabird populations, herring gulls are expanding their range. They currently breed from Alaska, northern Canada, and Greenland to as far south as the Carolinas.

Many kinds of gulls do not mate until they are three, four, or even five years old. Young birds are a mottled brown. As they get older, their dark feathers are gradually replaced by the familiar gray and white adult plumage.

Taxonomy

ORDER: *Charadriiformes*
FAMILY: *Laridae (gulls and terns)*
SUBFAMILY: *Larinae (gulls). Although "seagull" is the name we often give to any large, white birds we see along the coast, ornithologists recognize over forty distinct species of gulls in the world.*
SOME SPECIES:
Larus argentatus (herring gull), Larus delawarensis (ring-billed gull), Larus marinus (greater black-backed gull)

Feathers

All birds have feathers covering their bodies. Next time you are near a live bird, take a close look at the way its feathers are arranged on its body, and see how it uses them when it flies or perches. You can also study feathers that you find on the ground or in museum collections.

The bright feathers of this male goldfinch may help him attract a mate.

How feathers function

Feathers are lightweight, strong, and flexible. They function, or work, in several different ways. Feathers keep a bird's body warm and dry without adding a lot of weight. Overlapping layers of feathers contribute to the streamlined shape of a bird's body, helping it to move through the air or water more easily. A bird's wing and tail feathers enable it to fly, and to control the direction and speed of its flight.

The color and pattern of a bird's feathers can help other birds tell whether or not it belongs to their species, or whether it is a male or a female. Feathers help birds communicate about other matters, as well.

Many male birds have brightly colored feathers that they **display**, or "show off," to attract a mate, or to warn other males away from their territories. Peacocks rustle their feathers when they are courting peahens; a few other species also use feather sounds during courtship.

Feathers that blend in with a bird's surroundings can help protect it from predators. Scientists call this **protective coloration**. Precocial chicks often have down that makes them almost invisible against the ground. In species where females do most of the incubating or caring for young, females are often protectively colored, while males have brighter feathers used during courtship or territorial displays.

This duckling's down keeps it warm and dry even in cold water.

Perching birds use their tail feathers to help them balance on a branch.

Overlapping feathers help this cormorant move through the air and water more smoothly.

Kinds of feathers

Birds have many kinds of feathers. The **contour feathers** cover the bird's body surface. Underneath the contour feathers is the **down**. Down feathers are small and fluffy, and trap a lot of air; this makes them good insulators. Birds have other kinds of feathers, too.

Contour feathers *have a stiff* **rachis** *and interlocking* **barbs** *to keep them flat and smooth.*

Semiplumes *are fluffy like down, but they have a rachis running through the middle like contour feathers do.*

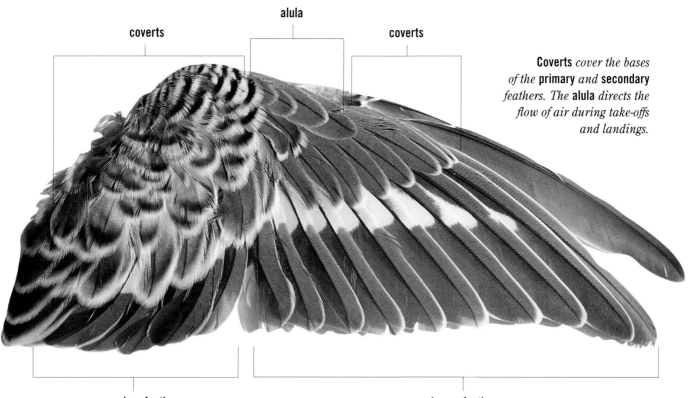

coverts

alula

coverts

Coverts *cover the bases of the* **primary** *and* **secondary** *feathers. The* **alula** *directs the flow of air during take-offs and landings.*

31

secondary feathers

primary feathers

Molting

As birds fly, hunt for food, and go about their other activities, their feathers become worn and damaged. Eventually, these old feathers fall out, and new ones grow in their place. Ornithologists refer to the loss and replacement of feathers as **molting**. Some birds molt their feathers once a year, while other birds molt more often. Some birds molt many of their feathers—including all of the flight feathers—in a relatively short period of time. This leaves them unable to fly for a few weeks, until a new set of flight feathers

grows in. Ducks molt in this manner, and the males of many duck species molt the bright-colored feathers of their **breeding plumage** before they lose their flight feathers. This way, they are protectively colored during the period when they can't fly. Many other species depend on flight in order to find food and escape predators. These birds molt over a much longer period of time, and lose their flight feathers one or two at a time. When large birds like crows and vultures fly overhead, you can sometimes see the place where a primary flight feather is missing.

Woodpeckers are always able to fly, for they molt their flight feathers gradually. Here, a new flight feather is growing in.

Preening

In order to stay warm and dry, and be able to fly, a bird must keep its feathers in good shape. **Preening** is one way birds take care of their feathers.

Feather care

If you have ever seen a bird rub or scratch itself with its beak, you have probably seen a bird preening. When a bird preens, it runs its beak through its feathers, which smooths and "reorganizes" them. Most birds rub oil over their feathers when they preen. This makes the feathers water-repellant, so they will not get soaked when the bird swims or gets rained on. A bird gets the oil by pressing its bill against an oil gland at the base of its tail. The bill gets oily, so when the bird rubs its bill against its feathers, the oil rubs off on them.

Birds have other ways to take care of their skin and feathers. They bathe in birdbaths, puddles, and ponds. This helps keep their feathers clean. Birds sometimes take dust baths, too. Though rolling around on the ground seems as if it would just get their feathers dirty,

Watch birds that are preening and bathing. See if you can tell whether they always go about it in the same way. Check to see if they preen at certain times of day, or after particular activities.

dust baths may help control parasites, like mites, lice, and fleas, that live on a bird's feathers and skin. Some birds even pick up ants and cigarette butts and rub them into their feathers. This behavior, called **anting**, may help control parasites or it may feel soothing to the skin.

*Most birds have an oil gland called the **uropygial gland** near the base of their tails. (Cormorants, and some other species, lack this gland.)*

Feathers up close

You can get a better sense of how preening works if you try to preen a feather yourself, with your fingers. Knock the feather against something, or ruffle it with your fingers, and you'll see breaks and gaps appear along the sides. You can repair these breaks by running the feather through your fingers. If you look at a feather with a hand lens or microscope, you can see how a feather is constructed. This will help you understand just what bird bills (or your fingers) do during preening. Contour feathers are made of many parallel strands, called **barbs**, that branch off of the central stem, or **rachis**. If you look closely at one barb, you will see smaller parallel strands, called **barbules**, along each side. The barbules have tiny hooks or teeth along each side. When a feather is smoothed out, these hooks on one barbule catch in the teeth of the one next to it, "zipping" the barbs together. When a feather is rumpled or bumped, some of the teeth "unzip," creating little breaks and gaps.

ZIPPED

UNZIPPED

Some feathers, like down feathers and semi-plumes, do not have interlocking barbules. These feathers look fluffy. Some birds have contour feathers that zip together in some places, but not in others. For example, great horned owls lack interlocking barbules along the edges of their flight feathers. This makes the tips of these feathers very soft, and allows them to move silently through the air.

33

DOWN ON THE FARM

A farm visit will give you a chance to observe the behavior of common domestic birds, that is, birds that are raised by people as a source of feathers, eggs, or meat. Turkeys, ducks, geese and guinea fowl are some of the birds you might see on a farm, but the most common is the domestic chicken.

Guinea fowl

34

Chicken habits and history

The jungle fowl of Southeast Asia, *Gallus gallus*, is the ancestor of our common domestic chicken.

Chickens have been selectively bred for so long that there are now many different breeds, or varieties. Some grow fast, and put on a lot of weight in the first few months of their lives. These breeds are raised for meat. Other kinds are good egg producers.

Farmyard chickens will eat any grain and table scraps they are fed. They also eat insects, worms, seeds, and the tender green shoots of new plants. Watch them as they walk around the farmyard and forage for food. They will peck at the ground with their

beaks, and use their large, strong feet to scratch up food.

Hens and roosters

Roosters, or cockerels, are adult male chickens. Female chickens are called hens if they have been laying eggs for over a year, and pullets during the first year they lay. You can tell hens and roosters apart by looking at their combs, tails, feet, and the way they hold their bodies.

Getting eggs

Farmers keep many more hens than roosters. In fact, some only keep hens. Since hens will lay eggs whether or not they mate with a rooster, it is not necessary to keep a rooster in order to get eggs to eat. A hen must mate with a rooster in order to lay fertilized eggs that will hatch into new chicks. Some people keep a rooster in the

Roosters often have larger combs than hens and pullets do, with longer folds of skin hanging below their beaks. Hens and pullets have fairly short tail feathers, while roosters have long plumes. Hens have heavier-looking bodies than roosters do. Roosters look as if they are craning their necks and sticking their chests out.

A strict pecking order determines the rank of every chicken in the flock.

flock so that there will always be some new chicks coming along to replace the birds they use for food.

A pullet will begin laying eggs when she is about six months old. Laying hens and pullets often lay an egg a day during the long days of spring and summer. In the winter, when days are short, they lay fewer eggs. Some people put an electric light in the hen house to keep egg production high year round. A hen will stop laying eggs entirely for a month or two each year when she molts. Chickens often molt in the fall. A hen will lay about two hundred eggs a year when she is young. After she is about three years old, she doesn't lay as many, and she is usually butchered.

The pecking order

The chickens in a flock are not all on "equal footing." One bird dominates the others. This dominant bird will peck at other chickens, and keep them away from any food it has found. It may also claim the best roost, or resting place. A second chicken follows the dominant bird in the pecking order. It responds to the dominant bird as "boss," but will peck and chase away the rest of the flock. This pattern continues down to the last bird in the pecking order, although the last bird, of course, has no one to dominate. If you watch a group of chickens as they forage for food, you will probably be able to figure out which birds are at the bottom of the pecking order, and which ones dominate the flock.

Behavior to look for

- feeding
- preening
- aggressive behavior (one bird chases or pecks at another)
- dust bathing
- mating (When a hen and rooster mate, the hen squats on the ground, and the rooster climbs up on her back. For a moment the cloacas of the two birds touch, and the rooster's sperm can pass into the hen's body. A bird's cloaca is the opening through which wastes are excreted, and through which eggs or sperm pass.)
- brooding (A brooding hen will gather her chicks under her body and wings to keep them warm.)

Hatching Chickens

Bird eggs will only hatch if they are kept at the proper temperature. In the wild, adult birds care for their eggs in various ways. Some birds, like the Egyptian plover, bury their eggs in the sand to keep them from getting too hot. Others, like the American robin, sit on their eggs to incubate them, or keep them warm. The emperor penguin carries its single egg about on its feet, incubating it under a fold of belly skin. If you want to hatch baby birds, you will need an incubator and some fertilized eggs. Domestic chicken eggs are usually the easiest to come by.

Setting up an incubator

An **incubator** is a special box that can be kept warm inside with a heating cable. Incubators are expensive, so check to see if a local school, nature center, or Cooperative Extension Service has one you can borrow. If you can't borrow one, see p. 62 for information on ordering one from a supply house.

Set up your incubator in a draft-free area, away from direct sunlight. Place a thermometer on the wire platform in the bottom of the incubator, so you can monitor the temperature inside.

Plug in the incubator the day before you pick up the eggs, so that the climate inside the incubator can stabilize. Check the incubator frequently during the day, so you can adjust the temperature and humidity if necessary. Chicken eggs are incubated at 100–101 degrees F. If your thermometer registers a warmer or cooler temperature, adjust the

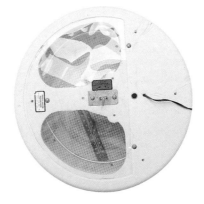

With a heating cable and some water, this incubator simulates the moist warmth of a hen's nest.

control on the thermostat. Moisture is also important for developing eggs, so put a pan of water under the wire platform to humidify the air. Once the temperature and humidity in the incubator have stabilized within the proper range, you are ready to add the eggs.

Getting eggs

You will need fresh, **fertile** chicken eggs to put in your incubator. Grocery store eggs won't do, because they are usually not fertile. The hens that laid them did not mate with roosters, so chicks will never develop inside these eggs. You may be able to get fertile eggs at a farm. If you don't live near a farm, call a local museum, nature center, or Cooperative Extension Service to find out where you can get eggs. If you do not have space at home to raise a flock of chickens, make arrangements for the chicks before you buy eggs. The farmer who sold you the eggs may be happy to raise the chickens.

Incubating the eggs— the first 18 days

Chicken eggs take 21 days to hatch. During this period, hens spend a lot of time sitting on their eggs to keep them warm. They also roll the eggs around with their beaks every now and then, which keeps the developing **embryos** from sticking to the **membrane**, or skin-like material that lines the shell. You will need to turn the eggs in your incubator, too. Simply open the incubator, and roll each egg over. If you mark each egg with a pencil "X" on one side, it will be easy to make sure you have turned all of the eggs completely. Turn the eggs three or four times a day until the 18th day of incubation—then leave them alone! They need to sit still during the three days before hatching.

Check the temperature and humidity before you open the incubator to turn the eggs. If the temperature drops even a few degrees below 100, the embryos will develop slowly. If the temperature rises above 103 degrees, they may be killed. Adjust the thermostat and water pans as necessary.

Days 19–21

During the last few days of incubation, you will need to care differently for the eggs. Each chick embryo will have moved into a hatching position within its eggshell, with its head at the large end of the egg. It is important to stop turning the eggs at this point, so the position of the chicks will not be disrupted. Leave the incubator closed at all times, so it will stay humid.

Don't forget to turn your eggs, or they won't develop properly.

On the 21st day, start looking for signs of hatching. You may hear peeping sounds coming from inside an egg, or notice a tiny hole in the middle of an eggshell. A **pipping** chick will push at the eggshell with its **egg tooth**, and crack little holes around its middle. Eventually, the chick will push the two halves of the eggshell apart and be free of them.

Some chicks take many hours to hatch, and it is tempting to open the incubator and help them! However, it is important to leave the incubator closed, and let the chicks do their

own work. That way, you won't accidentally hurt a tiny chick by handling it, and the air in the incubator will stay warm and moist, so the chicks will not stick to their eggshells.

Leave each chick in the incubator until it looks dry and fluffy. Then you can take it out of the incubator and move it to a **brooder** that is warmed to about 90 degrees by a 60 watt light bulb. Keep an eye on the chicks in the brooder to see how they are managing. If they constantly huddle under the light, they may be too cold, and you will need to adjust the light to bring it closer to the box. If the chicks avoid the light completely, the box may be too hot. Feed young chicks starter mash from a feed store or corn meal, and make sure their waterer is always full.

Move your chicks to a brooder once they are dry.

NESTING

Nests help adult birds keep their eggs and young warm and safe from predators. Small birds tend to make more elaborate, finely woven nests than larger birds do.

Selecting a site

In some species, the male of a pair decides where to build the nest, while in others, it is the female. Some pairs of birds actually look for possible nest sites together, though the female makes the final decision about where to build. Good nest sites are close to food and nest-building materials. They offer some protection from predators, and from wind, rain, and sun. Birds often compete for the best nest sites. A kestrel or starling may chase a flicker away from the cavity it has chiseled in a tree, and nest in the cavity itself. Herring gulls often spread their nests across the high ground of an island, leaving the smaller laughing gulls no alternative but to nest in low–lying, more frequently flooded areas when they arrive on the breeding grounds later in the spring. A good nest site can increase the chance that a bird's eggs and young will survive.

STARLING NEST

Building

Birds construct their nests in different ways. Some carry large twigs and sticks to the nest site with their feet. As the twigs pile up, the birds push at them with their feet and tug at them with their bills. This tangles the twigs to hold the nest

OSPREY NEST

Like other gulls, these black-legged kittiwakes often nest in colonies.

together, and it also shapes the nest. Some birds use their own sticky saliva to anchor nest materials in place, while others scoop up mouthful after mouthful of mud, and use it to build a sturdy foundation for their nest, or to cement it to the wall of a cave or building. Many birds carry grasses and plant fibers to their nest sites in their beaks. They secure these materials to a twig or branch with sticky spider webs and insect silk they have collected. As new materials are added, more silk is gathered to hold them in place. These birds use their beaks and bodies to shape their nests. They turn around and around in the middle of the nest, pushing at it with their feet, breasts, necks, or beaks. Eventually, this forms a cup–shaped hollow that can hold the eggs and young. A few birds are-actually able to weave plant fibers together with their beaks, and create elaborate, hanging nests.

Nest know-how

Adult birds do not teach their young how to make nests. Yet, when the young are old enough to mate and nest themselves, they build nests typical of their species. Scientists use the word instinctive to describe behavior that animals know without being taught. Instinct alone does not determine what a bird's nest will look like, however. Nests built by different members of a species may vary. For instance, ospreys usually nest off the ground in trees or on nest platforms, but on islands free from rats and other ground-dwelling predators, they may nest right on the beach. Orioles tend to weave their nests out of plant fibers, but if yarn or string is readily available, they'll make use of it. Birds that weave complicated nests may need practice before they are able to build a successful one.

All kinds of nests

Not all birds build elaborate nests. Some, like the common tern, *Sterno hirundo*, and the American oystercatcher, *Haematopus palliatus*, simply scrape a shallow depression on the ground, and lay their eggs in it. The great horned owl, *Bubo virginianus*, lays its eggs in an empty nest made by a crow, eagle, hawk, heron, or squirrel.

The common starling, *Sternus vulgaris*, will nest in natural cavities, woodpecker holes, and other protected spaces. Starlings pack grass, weeds, twigs, feathers, and other materials into the space until it is well filled. If the space is small, only a little material is needed, but if the space is large, the birds may transport bushels of nest material in their effort to fill it. Starlings are found throughout the eastern United States and midwest. Where they are present in large numbers, they may claim many of the available nest sites, making it difficult for bluebirds and other cavity nesters to build.

The Carolina wren, Thryothorus ludovicianus, is a tiny bird that makes a large, bulky nest with a side entrance. Dead leaves, weeds, twigs, strips of bark, shed snake skins, and other materials make up the nest. Fine material, such as grass, hair, and moss, lines the inside. Carolina wrens will nest in natural cavities, woodpecker holes, and birdhouses; they will also build under eaves, porches, and bridges. A female will lay four to eight eggs, and incubate them for two weeks.

Watching Nests

Next time you spot a bird carrying grass or a twig in its beak, watch to see where the bird goes. You may be able to locate the nest it is building. Keep track of the nest over the season to see how the adult bird cares for its young.

Observing an active nest

Start looking for active nests in the spring. Check around your home or school building—some birds nest under eaves and ledges, over doorways, and in other protected nooks and crannies. Once you locate a nest, observe it often. Try to move slowly and quietly when you are near the nest, and keep your distance at first. Some nesting birds are easily disturbed by people, and may abandon their eggs if they feel threatened by your visit. Binoculars will allow you to observe these birds from a safe distance. Few birds will abandon their chicks once the eggs have hatched.

Ornithologists use special, long-handled mirrors to get a look at nests they can't see from the ground. You can make your own nest-viewer by attaching a dime-store mirror to a pole or broom handle. Fasten the mirror securely so it will not fall off and break, or slip and bump a nest when you are using it. Try looking at abandoned nests, tree branches, and other high objects before you attempt to view an active nest. It may take some practice to learn to position the mirror so

you can see exactly what you want to.

You can make brief nest observations with your mirror whenever the adult birds have flown off to get food. If an adult is actually on its nest, **incubating** the eggs, or waiting nearby with food for the chicks, save your mirror for another time so that the adult can continue to take care of its young.

What's in a nest?

It is fascinating to see how different species of birds construct their nests, and what materials they use to make them. Start looking for abandoned nests to study in late fall, when birds no longer need them. You may be able to see many of the nest materials that were used by inspecting the surface of a nest. You can also take a nest apart bit by bit,

A piece of string, a bit of green cellophane, and some red wool were woven into this nest of twigs and grasses.

and take a more exact inventory. Sort the materials into piles, and see if there are any you can recognize. Take a small sample from each pile back to the area where you found the nest, and see if you can find a place where the nest-maker might have collected it. Some birds make many trips to a particular area to gather the materials they need for their nests.

The red-eyed vireo builds a hanging nest in the fork of a slender, horizontal branch.

Identifying nests

If you were able to observe a nest when it was active, you can simply identify the nest by identifying the birds you saw using it. If you spot a nest for the first time after it has been abandoned, a field guide or a key to the nests typically found in your area may help you figure out what kind of bird made it. Make sure to note the location of the nest. Some birds are particular about their nest sites, and tend to build in certain kinds of trees, or at a certain

height. Also look to see what the nest is made of, what its basic shape is, and whether it is loosely constructed or finely woven. If it is attached to a plant or building, look to see how it is attached. It may also help to measure the height of the nest, the depth of the cup, the **outside diameter** (the distance across the entire nest), and the **inside diameter** (the distance from one side of the hollow cup to the other). You can compare these measurements to those given in your field guide.

Studying nests

You can learn a lot from studying abandoned nests up close. However, in the United States, it is against federal regulations to collect the nest of any migratory bird or endangered species.

Educators, scientists, and other people who are interested in birds often obtain special permits to collect and study nests, feathers, or live birds. They can often provide you with nests to study. You can also contact the U.S. Fish and Wildlife Service in your area to find out if you will need a permit for your work.

Brood Parasites

Parasites are animals that live in or on other animals. Usually, the activities of a parasite harm its host in some way. Some birds are **brood parasites**. Instead of building nests and caring for their own young, they lay their eggs in the nests of other birds.

The brown-headed cowbird

The brown-headed cowbird, *Molothrus ater*, is a common brood parasite throughout most of the United States and many parts of Canada.

After a pair of cowbirds mate, the female goes off in search of nests to lay her eggs in.

Adult male cowbird

Timing is critical. She must find nests just as the host birds are ready to lay their own eggs, so that she can add her eggs to theirs. Then, her eggs will stand the best chance of being incubated and hatched. If she adds an egg to a clutch that has already been incubated for a week or so, the host's young will hatch well before her own egg is ready to. The host bird will start leaving the nest to find food for her young, and the cowbird egg may never hatch.

When a female cowbird finds a suitable nest, she will add an egg to the clutch it contains. Sometimes she will remove one of the host's eggs as well. Then, she will go on to lay another egg in a different nest. A brown-headed cowbird's first clutch of the season may contain six or more eggs, scattered in as many nests. A few days after she has completed her first clutch, a cowbird may begin on a second. Over one season, she may produce up to four clutches, or a total of 10-40 eggs.

This juvenile cowbird was hatched and raised in the nest of another kind of bird.

Hosting a cowbird

Some brood parasites only deposit eggs in the nests of closely related species, but brown-headed cowbirds are not so particular. Their eggs have been found in over 200 different kinds of nests, and over 100 species of birds have actually hatched and raised cowbird young. These hosts react differently to the presence of cowbird eggs in their nests. Some will notice a strange egg, and push it out. Others cover the egg with nest material, build a new nest on top of the old, and begin a new clutch. Still others abandon their nests. Sometimes, however, the host incubates the parasite's egg along with its own, and feeds the chick once it hatches.

If you ever notice a tiny sparrow or warbler feeding a chick much larger than itself, you can bet the chick is a cowbird. A cowbird egg hatches after 11-12 days of incubation. In some cases, the host's eggs have a slightly longer incubation period, and so the cowbird chick hatches first. Even when it hatches at the same time as its nest mates, the cowbird chick grows quickly and may soon outsize them. This gives it an edge when it comes to getting food from its foster parents.

Coast-to-coast cowbirds

One hundred and fifty years ago, the cowbird had a much more restricted range than it does today. Cowbirds lived only in the Great Plains region of the United States, where they followed herds of buffalo. They hopped through the grass, eating insects stirred up as the buffaloes walked and grazed, and ate ticks right off the buffaloes' backs. As the forests to the north, east, and west were cleared and farmed, new cowbird habitat was opened up.

Parasite control

Although the nesting habits of cowbirds may cause problems for individual birds, for the most part, these parasites do not endanger other species. This is not surprising, since a parasite that actually eliminated its hosts would have trouble surviving itself. Brown-headed cowbirds are **obligatory parasites**. They have lost the tendency or ability to nest and rear young themselves, and are actually dependent on other birds for their survival.

Taxonomy

ORDER: *Passeriformes*
FAMILY: *Emberizidae (black-birds, orioles, cowbirds, and meadowlarks)*
SUBFAMILY: *Icteridae*
GENUS AND SPECIES: *Molothrus ater. The bronzed cowbird, Molothrus aeneus, of Arizona, New Mexico, and south central Texas, is also a nest parasite.*

43

Raising a cowbird can be quite a job! This song sparrow is actually smaller than its giant "child."

Warblers

Some warblers are easy to recognize by their songs. Male yellowthroats utter a loud, fast "wichity-wichity-wichity-witchity-wit" throughout the breeding season. Females do not sing.

Wood warblers, the birds that make up the family *Parulidae*, are small songbirds with straight, slender bills. Most eat insects. Many warblers are brightly colored, especially male warblers in their breeding plumage. Look for warblers in brushy areas and in the woods.

Yellowthroats

The yellowthroat, *Geothlypis trichas*, breeds throughout much of North America. Males, females, and young birds all have bright yellow throats, and adult males have black bandit-style face masks that make them easy to recognize.

In the spring, male yellowthroats establish **territories**, or areas of land that they try to keep other yellowthroats out of. They often choose weedy, shrubby areas in marshes and other wet places. A territory may be an acre or two in size, but if there isn't much suitable habitat available, males may establish much smaller territories. A male establishes his territory partly by singing. He sings loudly from different perches within the territory he has chosen, and this warns other male yellowthroats to keep out. If another male yellowthroat does perch near by, the first male may dart about and flick his tail and wings, or give a harsh call. Neighboring males work out the boundaries of their "private property" through this language of movement and song.

Female yellowthroats join males in their territories and start nesting. A female usually builds a nest in a clump of weeds on or near the ground, and lays three to five tiny eggs in it. You could easily overlook a nest and walk right past it, but if you observe the behavior of the adult birds, you may get clues about where the nest is. They will call repeatedly if you walk near the nest, and will refrain from entering the nest with food if they notice you nearby. If you see a yellowthroat perched with an insect in its mouth, search the area for its nest.

Yellowthroat eggs hatch just about twelve days after the female begins incubating them. At first the young are blind, naked, and weak, but in a little over a week they are ready to leave the nest! They leave before they are able to fly. They walk and perch on weeds near the nest, and their parents continue to feed them. Once they are able to fly, they can follow their parents around. The young begin to find their own food about two or three weeks after they leave the nest.

It takes a lot of energy for a bird to establish and maintain a territory, but there are also benefits. Birds that secure territories with suitable nest sites and plenty of food may be better able to find food, attract a mate, and raise young.

Hybrids

The blue-winged warbler, *Vermivora pinus*, breeds throughout the midwest and the eastern United States, and winters from Mexico to Panama. Look for them in forest

Yellow warblers and other warblers are often parasitized by cowbirds.

Blue-winged warbler

edges and clearings, in undergrowth, and in fields that are becoming overgrown with saplings. A blue-winged warbler will sometimes mate with a golden-winged warbler, *Vermivora chrysoptera*. The offspring that result do not look quite like either parent. Ornithologists call these offspring **hybrids**; they occur when two closely related species **interbreed**. Although we tend to think that a fixed number of species live on our planet, in fact, species continually change, or **evolve**, over time. Blue-winged warblers and golden-winged warblers probably evolved from a single species, and their behavior and bodies are still similar enough that they sometimes interbreed.

The yellow warbler, *Dendroica petechia*, breeds in most parts of the United States and many parts of Canada. Look for them in bushes, gardens, thickets, suburban shrubbery, and along swamp edges and streams. Both males and females are more yellow than other kinds of warblers. Males have rusty streaks on their breasts. Females have faint streaks, or plain yellow breasts. Yellow warblers are common, and they defend small territories, so you will find their behavior easier to study than some other species.

Taxonomy

ORDER: *Passeriformes*
FAMILY: *Parulidae (wood warblers–small {4-6 inch} birds with straight, slender bills)*
SOME GENERA:
* *Vermivora (includes V. chrysoptera, the golden-winged warbler, and V. pinus, the blue-winged warbler)*
* *Dendroica (tree-dwelling warblers with wingbars and tail spots; includes D. petechis, the yellow warbler)*
* *Geothlypis (includes the yellowthroat, G. trichas)*

Bird Songs and Calls

The sounds birds make are a familiar—and often beautiful—part of our daily lives, and they have special meaning for many people. Flocks of honking geese tell us winter is on the way, and forecast spring's return. Owls can sound spooky, and mourning doves sad. Bird sounds are a form of communication. However, the meaning they have for us can be quite different from the meaning they carry for birds! It takes careful watching and listening, as well as some imagination, to figure out what a bird is "saying."

Calls and songs

Birds make different kinds of sounds. Calls are usually short, simple sounds, and they are made by males, females, and young birds. An individual can make a variety of different calls, and each sends a particular message to other birds. When a nestling peeps, for example, its parents feed it. The peeping seems to say "Feed me!" Ducklings often call as they swim or walk near their mother, and their mother calls back. These calls probably help a family of ducks stay in touch with one another, as if each member were continually saying "Here I am—over here." If one duckling gets separated from the group, it calls more loudly and frequently. Its mother responds to its **distress call** by coming near. The

honking calls of migrating Canada geese may serve a similar purpose—they help the members of a flock stay together, but not so near they might collide. Birds call at all times of the year. Their calls can help members of a family or flock recognize one another, sound an alarm when danger is near, or warn intruders away from a territory, perch, or feeding area. The "language" of a particular species may include as many as twenty–five distinct calls! Listen closely to the birds that are most common in your neighborhood, and see how many different calls you can recognize.

Bird songs are usually longer and more complicated than calls. Each species has a distinct song, and you can learn to recognize it by particular note patterns, or phrases, that are repeated each time the song is sung. You will hear different variations of a species' song, though, because one individual may sing a little differently than another, or sing many versions of the same basic song. Of course, a bird can recognize its species' song, too, and use it to identify members of its own species. Most singing birds are males. During the breeding season, a male's song may attract a mate, or help him establish and maintain his territory. Early in the season, some males spend half of each day singing, and repeat their songs over a thousand—or even two thousand—times! The females of some species also sing, but they do not sing as often as males do. In some species, males and females sing duets. Many birds seem to know their songs instinctively; they can sing the song typical of their species even if they have never heard it before. Others learn their songs.

Ways to learn about bird songs and calls

- Go for an early morning bird walk, and see how many different sounds you can hear. Try listening at other times of day, as well, for some birds are noisiest in the evening, or at night.
- Keep track of the time of year when you hear a particular song. This will help you learn when various species are breeding.
- When you hear a bird song or call, try to find the bird that made it. Watch to see how other birds nearby respond. Over time, you may be able to figure out what sounds are made by a particular species, and what they mean.
- Check out a tape recording of bird songs from your public library, or buy one. If you hear a familiar song, you can listen to find out what bird made it. You can look at a field guide as you listen to the tape, and match up the way birds look with the way they sound.

- Try making your own bird recordings with a portable tape recorder. You'll get the best results with nearby birds that make relatively loud sounds.
- Describe the bird songs you hear in a notebook. Some people find that putting words to bird songs helps them remember and recognize them. The white-throated sparrow sounds as if it's singing "Oh, Sweet, Canada Canada Canada" or "Oh, Sam, Peabody Peabody Peabody," while the Carolina wren says "Teacher teacher teacher," and the barred owl asks "Who cooks for you?"
- Some birds will respond when you imitate their songs with your voice or a wooden bird call. Birds may respond to tape recorded songs as well. (See page 62 for information on ordering wooden bird calls.)

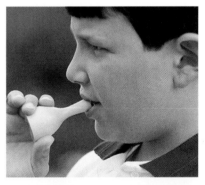

COLLECTIONS

Early naturalists and scientists who were interested in birds often collected birds to study. They shot birds and used them as models for drawings and paintings, or preserved them for other research. Eggs and nests were collected, too. Now, laws protect most birds and their eggs, and only researchers with special permits may collect them. The large collections made in earlier times are preserved in museums, universities, and nature centers. They are valuable resources for people who want to learn about birds.

Learning from museum collections

A museum visit can be helpful when you are learning to identify birds. Find a display of birds that live in your area, and try to identify them with a field guide. Then, compare your identification with the museum labels. You can also bring a sketch pad and pencil to a museum, and draw the birds you see. Unlike the birds you sketch in the field, museum specimens stand still! You will be able to capture many details of their appearance in your drawing.

Bird specimens that have been prepared to look as lifelike as possible are called mounts. Museums usually put their bird mounts on display, because they give visitors the best sense of what birds look like in the wild. Bird specimens can also be made into study skins. When a study skin is made, the bird's wings are folded against its body, and its neck, back, and tail are placed in line. Study skins don't look as natural as mounts, but they are much easier to prepare, and they don't take up much space when they are stored. They are usually kept in drawers rather than put on display. The drawers are arranged by orders, families and genera so that when a researcher or student is interested in a specific species or group of birds, they are easy to find. If you are studying a particular kind of bird and do not see it displayed in the museum or nature center you visit, ask if there are study skins that someone on the staff will show you.

Many museums also have extensive collections of bird eggs. Since you may only get to see a few kinds of bird eggs in the wild, egg collections can

help you find out what other eggs look like. Egg collections have also provided researchers with important information. For example, they helped researchers figure out that the pesticide DDT was causing hawks and eagles to lay eggs with thin, easily broken shells. Measurements taken from museum specimens collected before DDT was introduced had much thicker shells than eggs that were laid afterwards. Egg collecting was once a popular hobby, but now laws designed to protect birds prohibit it.

Making your own collection

Most wild birds are protected by special laws. These laws prohibit people from collecting live birds, or their feathers, nests, or eggs. Such laws may seem unnecessarily strict; after all, it doesn't harm a bird if you collect a nest it has abandoned or a feather it has molted! However, in 1918 when the Migratory Bird Treaty Act was passed, very strict laws were needed. Hunting and collecting had caused several species of birds to become extinct, and others were endangered. Making it illegal to own even feathers and other bird parts made it less likely that people would kill birds.

If you want to make your own collection of bird nests or feathers, you will need to apply for a special permit from the U. S. Fish and Wildlife Service, or work with an adult who already has a permit. Call the Fish and Wildlife office in your area for more information. You can collect feathers from domestic and pet birds without a permit. You can also collect broken eggshells you find on the ground. Store your eggshells in plastic boxes or empty egg cartons lined with cotton. Use a field guide to nests and eggs to help you identify any you don't recognize, or compare them with museum specimens.

Bringing Back Bluebirds

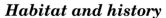he Eastern Bluebird, *Sialia sialis*, can be found in the United States and southern Canada, east of the Rockies. Look for bluebirds perching on fence posts, telephone wires, and tree stumps near roadsides, in orchards, and in open woodlands.

Habitat and history

Eastern bluebirds are adapted for life in a particular kind of environment. They need cavities to nest in, but since they cannot chisel their own cavities, they must find decaying trees with natural cavities or abandoned woodpecker holes to use. Bluebirds also need plenty of open land where they can find insects and berries to eat.

Before European settlers arrived in North America, most Eastern bluebirds probably lived in forest clearings created by high winds, or in woods that had been burned by forest fires. The dead and decaying trees in these areas provided nest sites, and the short ground cover made for good hunting. As settlers cleared land for farms, they created more bluebird habitat, and bluebirds became one of our most common

songbirds. By the 1930's, however, researchers noted that bluebird populations were declining. By the 1960's, bluebirds were uncommon in most of the northeastern states.

Why the decline?

Eastern bluebirds became scarce for many reasons. As farmland and orchards gave way to cities and suburbs, the habitat available to them shrank. Land use practices such as clearing away dead or dying trees, replacing wooden fence posts with metal ones, and successful prevention of forest fires eliminated nest sites. Competition for remaining nest sites increased as house sparrows and starlings (two cavity-nesting species introduced to the United States from Europe during the mid-1800s) became common. Periods of severe weather and the

heavy use of chemical pesticides like DDT affected bluebirds, too.

Reestablishing bluebirds

People in many areas are trying to reestablish bluebirds in areas where they once were common. At the Myles Standish State Forest in Massachusetts, researchers from the Manomet Bird Observatory and the Massachusetts Division of Fisheries and Wildlife are trying to learn more about bluebirds so that conservation and management efforts can be succeed.

Researchers study bluebirds in a part of the forest that has been mostly cleared of trees. The remaining trees and shrubs provide perches for bluebirds to hunt from, and a few nest sites.

Male Eastern bluebirds can be recognized by their blue backs and wings, rusty breasts, and white bellies. Females have much grayer backs, and young birds have spotted breasts.

Each spring, researchers put up 30–40 nest boxes to provide additional nest sites. Professional and volunteer researchers monitor these boxes, or check them frequently. They record the number of eggs found in each nest, and keep track of how many nestlings survive and **fledge**. When a nest **fails**, or does not produce healthy fledglings, researchers try to figure out why.

Over the years, researchers have learned some things that have helped them insure the success of nesting bluebirds. They have found it is important to clean old nest material out of the boxes once the nesting season is over, because when birds reuse old nests, they are often seriously troubled by parasites. Researchers also found that more bluebirds may nest in the study area when boxes are put up in pairs. When single boxes were put

up, many were claimed by tree swallows. Many of the paired boxes are claimed by tree swallows, too, but since these birds are territorial, they will chase off any other tree swallows that try to nest in the box "next door." Tree swallows do not defend their territories against bluebirds, however, so once the swallows claim their nest boxes, bluebirds and other cavity nesters can have the "leftovers."

Female Eastern bluebirds usually lay four or five eggs, and incubate them for about two weeks. Often the eggs are blue, but sometimes they are white.

Forest fires— disasters or blessings?

Many fires have burned in Myles Standish State Forest over the centuries. These fires created an open, grassy woodland that provided many bluebirds with a suitable place to live. As fire prevention and control techniques improved, and fewer fires swept across the forest, the bluebird population declined. Certain species of plants and animals depend on the kind of habitat that a forest fire creates. There is no question that fires are destructive, but in their wake, new communities of plants and animals may flourish.

Taxonomy

ORDER: *Passeriformes*
FAMILY: *Turdidae*
(thrushes; this family also includes the robin, *Turdus migratorius*)
GENUS: *Sialia* (includes the Western bluebird, *Sialia mexicana,* and the mountain bluebird, *S. currucoides,* as well)
SPECIES: *Sialia sialis*

51

Feeding Birds

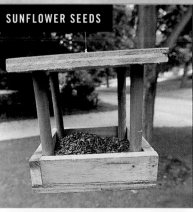

SUNFLOWER SEEDS

Birds are big eaters. Keeping warm in winter, flying, and nest building are activities that burn up a lot of calories! One way to get a good look at birds is to set up a feeding station. Birds are always on the lookout for new food supplies. Once they discover your feeding station, many will become regular visitors.

Setting up a station

First, decide where to locate your feeding station. If possible, put it where you can easily see it from your house or apartment. That way, it will be easy to maintain, and you will be able to observe the birds that visit whether you are indoors or out.

Next, decide what kind of feeders you will put up. There are dozens of different bird feeders on the market, and many more that you can build yourself. Some can be filled with seed and placed on a pole, or hung from a wire or window. Others hold **suet**, or fat. Still others are made to sit on the ground and hold cracked grain, crumbs, and seeds. Since birds have varied diets and feeding habits, you will attract the widest variety of species if you set up different kinds of feeders.

SUET

A simple feeding station can include:
- one hanging feeder full of sunflower seeds
- a lump of suet in an old plastic mesh onion bag
- cracked corn scattered on the ground.
- a piece of wood with holes filled with peanut butter

CRACKED CORN

Talk to neighbors who have managed to attract birds before you spend a lot of money buying new feeders. They may have found some that work particularly well, and are easy to clean. (You will need to clean out your feeders and wash them periodically, especially if rainy weather wets the food.) Once your station is established, you can experiment with different kinds of food and feeders to see which attract the most birds. Keep track of the species that visit each feeder. (For more information on ordering feeders, see p. 62.)

PEANUT BUTTER

52

Some food birds eat

- sunflower seeds
- other seeds, such as millet, oats, wheat, and safflower seeds
- cracked corn
- chopped nuts
- suet
- peanut butter
- fruit (orioles and tanagers are attracted to orange halves)
- sugar water (hummingbirds)
  These foods are available at grocery stores, feed stores, and from mail order companies.

Squirrel-proofing your station

Birds aren't the only animals that eat sunflower seeds and cracked corn! If you don't want squirrels and chipmunks to eat from your feeders, make sure to put them on metal poles instead of wooden ones, or hang them from a wire strung between two poles. This will make it difficult for squirrels and chipmunks to reach your feeders. You can also buy plastic "squirrel-bafflers" to fit many feeders. Of course, there's no way to keep squirrels away from the food you scatter on the ground, so see what you can learn about them when they come to eat.

Perches and hiding places

Birds are more likely to feed at your station if there are plenty of places nearby where they can perch, and places to take cover if a person, cat, or hawk surprises them. Fences, poles, shrubs, trees, and tall weeds can provide perches and cover. If your feeding station is in a bare or exposed area, try planting tall flowers or shrubs close by. Pound a few poles or fence posts into the ground, or scatter a few large, dead branches around. You can also prop large branches against a fence post to support them. They will provide food for woodpeckers and other birds that search tree bark for insects to eat, as well as offer places to perch.

Water

Birds need water as well as food. If you have an old birdbath, set it up at your station. If not, you can weight a shallow tray or garbage can lid with a rock, and keep it full of fresh water.

Hummingbirds feed on the nectar from flowers, but you can also attract them with sugar water.

IN AN OLD BARN

The structures we build sometimes make good nest sites for birds. An old barn may house swallows, barn owls, pigeons, starlings, and other species. If you don't live near a barn, look for birds in a garage, shed, or some other open building. If you see birds flying in and out of the windows, or a white-wash of droppings on the walls or rafters, you have probably found a building where birds nest.

Barns, garages and other open buildings can attract many kinds of birds.

The barn swallow, Hirundo rustica, *breeds through-out most of North America. You can recognize a barn swallow by its long, deeply forked tail, and rusty chin and forehead.*

These days, it is unusual to find a barn swallow nesting anywhere other than a structure made by peo-ple. Yet, barn swallows evolved long before the coun-tryside was dotted with sheds, barns, and bridges. Probably, barn swallows used to build their mud nests on cliffs and in caves. Occasionally, some still do.

Mouthfuls of mud

Barn swallows, *Hirundo rustica*, often nest togeth-er in groups, or colonies. It takes a pair of barn swallows about a week to build a nest. Mouthful by mouthful, they fetch mud from a nearby pond or river bank and pack it into place on the rough side of a rafter or some other surface the mud will stick to. They add pieces of straw or grass as they go, and finally, they line the nest with feathers. The finished nest is strong and heavy, and may be fixed up and used again next year. Once the nest is fin-ished, the female barn swallow lays four to six small, speckled eggs in it. She and her mate take turns incubating the eggs for about fifteen days, until they hatch.

Nests that are at least partly supported by a horizontal surface are safest. Nests built on vertical surfaces occasionally fall down, killing the eggs or young.

Caring for young

After the eggs have hatched, both parents must work full-time to catch enough insects to feed their growing young. It's fun to watch their acrobatic maneuvers as they swoop after mosquitoes, dragonflies, and other flying insects. Barn swallow nestlings need food at least four times an hour, all day long, just as other altricial chicks do. At night they rest, and are able to do without food. Flying insects are usually plentiful during the nesting season. During rainy weather, however, insects take cover, and so adult swallows are unable to feed their young. Long periods of stormy weather can be a serious problem for a swallow colony; many young may die of starvation.

Within three weeks of hatching, young barn swallows are ready to leave the nest. Some pairs of barn swallows will raise just one family each summer. Others raise a second brood after their first nestlings have fledged.

Housekeeping

You may find broken eggshells and fecal sacs scattered on the barn floor or just outside the door.

These broken eggshells and fecal sacs are good clues that birds are nesting overhead.

The fecal sacs are membranes that contain the young nestlings' wastes. Nestlings excrete these packages of wastes, and their parents carry them off. (When the nestlings grow older and stronger, they stop producing these packages, and simply defecate over the side of the nest as adult birds do.) Adult swallows use their beaks to carry debris away from their nests. The nests stay cleaner this way—but not the barn!

At summer's end

The barn swallows that began making nests in this Massachusetts barn in mid-April will be gone by the end of August. They will have started a migratory journey that may take them six thousand miles from their breeding grounds. Barn swallows breed throughout North America, and winter from Costa Rica south to Argentina. Individual barn swallows often return to the same spot year after year, so once you find a building where they nest, you can look forward to years of swallow-watching there.

55

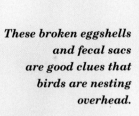

Taxonomy

ORDER: *Passeriformes*
**FAMILY: *Hirundinidae*
(swallows—graceful birds with small feet, long, pointed wings, and short bills with very wide gapes. Flying insects are the primary food of swallows.)**
**GENUS AND SPECIES:
Hirundo rustica
(barn swallow)**

Migration

Migrating Canada geese are strong fliers, and they travel both day and night. At times they interrupt their journeys to rest and eat.

Many birds spend the spring and summer months in one part of the world and winter somewhere else. The regular, seasonal journeys of these birds are called **migrations**. Some birds migrate from breeding grounds in the northern hemisphere to wintering areas below the equator. Other birds spend much of the year at sea, but move to coastal beaches and islands to nest and raise their young. Some birds migrate just a few hundred miles, while others fly thousands.

Traveling geese

In autumn, look and listen for Canada geese on their way south. They migrate in groups, or **flocks**, made up of separate families. They usually fly in a "V" formation or a long trailing line, honking as they go. Many people think that different geese take turns leading the flock, and that the lead goose drops to the back when it tires. Some ornithologists question this, however, because they have not seen such changes take place in the flocks they have studied. They suspect that one dominant goose may lead the flock for the entire migration.

Some flocks of Canada geese spend the winter as far north as southern Newfoundland; others fly south as far as Mexico. Canada geese have a strong "homing" instinct: flocks tend to winter in the same area year after year, and return to the same breeding grounds each spring. Some Canadas begin their northward migration as early as mid-January or February, while others remain on the wintering grounds into March.

Following flocks

For centuries people have known that some birds appear in certain places each spring, then disappear again in the fall. It was hard to be sure of anything more, though, because people didn't have a way to follow birds as they traveled. Then, in the 1920s, researchers began banding birds. Banding made it possible to identify individual birds, and learn something about where they go. It takes a long while to piece together the travels of a particular species from banding studies, however, because data rolls in so slowly. For every thousand birds that are banded, fewer than ten are ever recaptured! Over the years, ornithologists have developed other ways to keep track of flying birds. Some follow flocks by driving after them in cars, or flying after them in airplanes. Scientists can track flocks of birds using radar, or by attaching a tiny radio transmitter to an individual bird's back. None of these methods is perfect. Bird can fly places that cars cannot go, or fly beyond the range of a radio receiver. Researchers have been able to figure out the migration routes of most species, but there are still many details that no one is sure about.

How do they do it?

Scientists are not sure exactly how birds are able to find their way to particular breeding and wintering grounds—especially young birds that have never made the journey before. However, they have learned something about the kinds of information birds notice about their environment. It seems that some birds use the sun as a compass, and have some kind of "biological clock" that allows them to make adjustments as the sun moves across the sky. Others use the stars to steer by. In overcast weather, some birds may use the earth's magnetic field to navigate. Birds can also recognize land formations, and may have some kind of internal "map" that enables them to make use of what they see. Some researchers even think a bird's sense of smell may help it find its way from place to place.

Why migrate?

It uses up a lot of energy to fly thousands of miles; small birds may lose as much as forty percent of their body weight on a long migratory flight! Yet, migration may still benefit a bird, even though the costs of migration are high. Migratory birds are able to raise young in places where food is plentiful during the breeding season, but scarce during the winter. When weather turns harsh and their food supply dries up, migratory birds can take advantage of more favorable conditions elsewhere. Migratory birds can spend most of the year in places such as the open ocean where it would be impossible to raise young.

Taxonomy

ORDER: *Anseriformes*
FAMILY: *Anatidae (swans, geese, and ducks–waterfowl)*
GENUS: *Branta*
SPECIES: *Branta canadensis*

Canada Geese

The Canada goose, *Branta canadensis*, ranges across most of North America. Look for it in city parks, on fields and golf courses, and along rivers, lakes, bays, and marshes. Canada geese may be summer or winter residents in your area, or they may live near you year-round. All Canada geese have gray or brown backs and wings, and black legs and feet. They have a black head and neck with a white cheek patch, and a black bill. Ornithologists recognize many distinct races of Canada geese. Some are just a little larger than mallard ducks, while others measure 45 inches from bill to tail. These races often mix on wintering grounds, but breed in different areas.

Canada geese graze on clover and other green plants, and eat grain from wild plants and cropland. They also eat the roots, stems, and seeds of various aquatic plants.

BANDING BIRDS

Perhaps you have seen a bird with an aluminum bracelet, or band, around one leg. Bands can help scientists learn about the travels and habits of individual birds. Bright-colored plastic bands are used as well as metal ones. These allow researchers to spot particular birds at a distance.

How banding works

Each aluminum band has its own unique number stamped on it. When a person bands a bird, she records the number of the band she uses on a special form. She also lists the date, the location where the bird was banded, and its species, age, weight, and sex. The bird is then released, and its record is sent to a central office that collects information from bird banders all over the country. If the bird is ever captured again, the person who captures it will again record its band number, and the date and location of capture. This new record will also be sent to the central office. Ornithologists who are trying to learn about the distribution or migratory route of a species can get records, or data, about that species from the central office. Many thousands of birds are banded each year. However, relatively few banded birds are recaptured, or found dead, so information about their travels builds up slowly.

A bird in the hand

Banders use different techniques to catch birds. Some species are most easily banded as chicks, while they are still unable to fly. If the chicks are in a nest off the ground, the bander must climb up to the nest on a ladder, and gently remove the chicks from the nest one at a time. Once a chick is banded, it is returned to the nest. Large birds like herons, owls, and hawks are sometimes banded in this way. Ground nesting species, like gulls and terns, can also be banded as chicks.

Mist nets are useful for catching small perching birds. A mist net is made of very fine, strong thread, so that when it is strung up between two trees, it is barely visible. Birds flying though the area don't notice the net, and fly right into it. Banders remove each bird that is caught and place it temporarily into a cloth bag, where it stays until it is banded and then released. Mist nets must be checked frequently so that the birds do not have to spend a long time tangled in the net. Nets are closed up on rainy days or very hot ones, so that birds will not be subjected to harsh weather.

Steps in banding a bird

- Each bird that has flown into the mist net is gently untangled by the bander. The bander is particularly careful of the bird's legs, which can easily be broken if the bird is not handled properly.

- The bird is carefully identified. The bander determines whether it is a male or female, and whether it is an adult or juvenile, as well as what species it is. Wing measurements helped the bander decide that this red-winged blackbird was a juvenile, not a female.

- The bander checks the condition of the bird's body and feathers. Sometimes, when the breast feathers are gently blown, a large featherless area appears. This brood patch indicates that the bird is incubating eggs or raising young. Some birds lose many of their breast feathers when they start incubating. They are able to warm their eggs more easily this way, for there is no layer of insulating feathers between their warm bodies and their eggs.

- The bird is put head down into a special cone and weighed. The cone keeps it from flying off while it is being weighed. Birds often lose a great deal of weight when they are caring for eggs and young, then fatten up before they migrate.
- The bander decides what size band to use. The band must be the proper size, so it won't fall off or feel tight around the bird's leg.

- Special pliers are used to open the band, then close it around the bird's leg.
- Once the band number and other information have been recorded, the bird is released.

Legalities

It is illegal to catch and band birds unless you hold a special permit, or work for someone who does. If you would like to watch birds being banded, call a local university, nature center, or Audubon Society. If you notice that a bird in your schoolyard or at your feeder has a band on its leg, you don't need to do anything about it. But if you find a dead bird wearing a band, mail the band to the

Bird Banding Laboratory
U.S. Fish and Wildlife Service
12100 Beech Forest Road
Laurel, Maryland 20708-4037

Make sure to include your name and the location and date that you found the bird.

Bird Rehabilitation

Buffy Curtis is a wildlife rehabilitator. She cares for birds and other animals that have been injured or abandoned, then releases them as soon as they are able to survive on their own. Often her charges are young birds whose parents have been killed by cats.

A big towel helps keep this injured cormorant warm and dry.

Bird care

The first thing a rehabilitator needs to do with any newly acquired bird is make sure it is warm and dry. Nestlings that would normally be kept warm by their parents and a crowd of siblings sharing the same nest can be kept in a cage with a heating pad underneath it. Once they are fully feathered and able to walk around on their own, the heating pad can be removed. Young nestlings that are unable to stand will need a substitute nest to support their bodies. Some caretakers use a plastic berry box lined with tissues.

After the bird is warm and properly housed, it must be identified. Accurate identification is important, because different species of birds require different food. Buffy refers to a special key to help her identify nestlings and fledglings, since they do not look like the adult birds pictured in most field guides. Once she has identified a bird, she can make up a formula that imitates the diet it would get in the wild. Birds that eat a variety of plant and animal food get a mixture of softened monkey chow or puppy food, mixed with cooked carrots, wheat germ, cereal, and fruit. Insect-eating birds are fed insects blended with protein powder, acidophilus, hard-boiled egg, and chicken. At first, a baby bird must be fed every fifteen minutes during the day. As it gets older, it can eat larger quantities of food at a time, and wait longer between feed-

A young bird takes food from a popsicle stick.

ings. As the bird grows, its diet will change. It must learn to eat whatever food is typical for adults of its species before it can be released.

Captive birds must be kept clean. Wastes should be removed several times a day, and any food that is stuck to the beak or surrounding feathers after a feeding should be wiped off.

Rehabilitators must fight the urge to make the animals they care for into pets. Buffy does not pet or cuddle the baby birds she raises, or talk to them as she might a pet dog or cat. Instead, she makes little chirping noises as she feeds a nestling, to simulate the sounds its parents might have made while feeding. As the nestling matures, she moves it to an outdoor cage. Eventually, she begins leaving the cage open, so the bird can come and go. However, she continues to supply food and shelter until it is clear the bird can manage completely on its own.

Learning to care for wild animals

Some nature centers and wildlife trusts offer special courses in wildlife rehabilitation, and allow children to enroll along with a parent. If you want to learn more about caring for wild birds, check to see if such a course is taught in your area, or find out if there is a bird rehabilitator in your area that you can visit. Your local Audubon Society or the U.S. Fish and Wildlife Service may be able to help you find one. A person must hold a special permit in order to rehabilitate seabirds, shorebirds, and birds of prey. You can care for a smaller bird, though, if you get a permit for temporary possession of the bird from the Bureau of Sport Fisheries and Wildlife.

If you find a baby bird

If you find a baby bird on the ground, the best thing you can do for it is to return it to its nest. Its own parents can care for it far better than you can, and it is more likely to live to adulthood under their care than under yours. It is okay to

handle the bird gently in order to move it into its nest. Most birds have a poor sense of smell and will not abandon a chick just because it has been touched by a person. If you can't find the nest, gently put the bird in a cardboard box and place the box on a branch or bush near the place you found it. Make sure it is out of direct sunlight, and out of reach of neighborhood cats. Check your boxed bird later in the day. If hours go by and no adult bird comes to care for the chick, you can call a local rehabilitator, veterinarian, or Audubon Society for advice.

When young birds first leave their nests, their parents often travel with them and continue to feed them for a while. Many well-meaning people collect these young fledglings, assuming they have fallen from their nests, when actually, they are simply becoming more and more independent. You may see precocial chicks, like quail, plovers, and ducks, moving around without their parents when they are only a day old. Usually, their parents are nearby, even though you may not have noticed them. Make certain a baby bird has truly been abandoned before you collect and care for it.

The yellow gape at the corners of this bird's beak identify it as a youngster. Although it has left its nest, its parents have not abandoned it. They will continue to feed it until it is able to find food on its own.

Continuing

Once you get interested in birds, you'll find you notice them more and more. You'll also find you have more and more questions about them! Your own observations and records will help you think about the puzzling things birds do. There are also many people and organizations that can help you continue your study of ornithology.

Check the phone book to see if there is a chapter of the Audubon Society in your area. (It may be listed under the name of your state, rather than under "Audubon.") If you have trouble locating an Audubon Society, write or call

**National Audubon Society
700 Broadway
New York, NY 10003
1-800-274-2401**

Many communities also have birding clubs. The members of these clubs can help you identify birds, and they may let you attend some of their meetings and bird-watching trips.

Call nearby colleges, universities, and research centers to find out if there are any ornithologists, ecologists, or biologists on staff who can meet with you or answer questions by phone. Colleges and research centers often have extensive collections of study skins and bird's eggs and nests that you may be able to study. Many museums and nature centers also have good collections, and keep parts of these collections on permanent display.

Zoos are a good place to study birds from many parts of the world. Many zoos have aviaries you can walk through, and penguin or seabird exhibits. Some aquariums have penguins and seabirds on display, too. Pet stores can be good places to see birds, and pet store owners may know of people that breed birds who would be happy to discuss their work with you.

How to Order Equipment

The most enjoyable way to study birds is to go out on your own and find them, depending on where you live and the season. But some projects require special equipment that you can't make or find at home, such as binoculars, egg incubators, and field guides. Almost all of the equipment mentioned in *Ornithology* can be ordered through the mail or by phone from the Carolina Biological Supply Company. If you want to order by phone, you'll need an adult with a credit card. Just give the person on the phone the catalog number listed here with each item you want. Remember, a shipping and handling charge is added to each purchase.

IN THE EASTERN US
Carolina Biological Supply
2700 York Road
Burlington, NC 27215
Toll free: 1-800-334-5551

IN THE WESTERN US
Carolina Biological Supply
Box 187
Gladstone, OR 97027
Toll free: 1-800-547-1733

If you can't borrow a pair of Binoculars (p. 10-11) from a friend or your school, you can order a good 8 x 30 pair with a case for about $70.00 (catalog #60-2560); a 3x Hand Magnifier for examining small items only costs about $2.00 (cat.#60-2108). Any good local bookstore should carry Field Guides (pp. 14-15) to the birds in your area, but you can also order them. For a good beginner's guide, try *Birds* from Golden Guides ($3.95, cat.#45-5080). If you want a more advanced guide, try the Audubon Society's *Field Guide to Eastern Birds* (cat.#45-5096) or *Western Birds* (cat.#45-5096A), each for $15.95. The Peterson Field Guides to *Birds East of the Rockies* (cat.#45-5091, $16.95) and to *Western Birds* (cat.# 45-5092, $15.95) are also excellent. For anyone especially interested in bird behavior, the Stokes *Guide to Bird Behavior* (Vol. I, cat.# 45-5073, $9.95) is an excellent book. And if you want to learn a lot about bird nests, the Peterson Guide to *Bird's Nests* (cat.#45-5072A, $13.95) is very handy. Feathers (pp.30-31) are hard to find on your own, and Carolina doesn't sell them, but you might find them at your local art or crafts supply store. If you can't borrow an Incubator to hatch chicks in (pp.36-37), you can order one for about $50.00 (cat.#70-1194). Bird Feeders (pp.52-53) of many kinds are fun and easy to make, but you can also order them from Carolina, starting from about $10.00 (cat.#650-1801); hummingbirds need a special feeder for their liquid food, which you can order for about $15.00 (cat.#16-1822A). If you want to set up a Nesting Box of your own (pp. 50-51), you can order a kit from Carolina for about $7.00 (cat.#65-1936).

ATTENTION TEACHERS: *Most of the equipment and specimens here are available at quantity discounts for classroom use. In addition to Carolina Biological Supply, these supplies are also available from Science Kit and Boreal Laboratories (1-800-828-7777) and Ward Natural Science Establishment (1-800-962-2660).*

Glossary

altricial: young that are unable to see, feed themselves, or keep themselves warm after they hatch.

alula: a group of small feathers on a bird's wing that can direct air during takeoff and landing.

anting: an unusual behavior where a bird takes an ant in its beak, and rubs it over the feathers.

band: a small plastic or metal bracelet used to mark an individual bird so it can be identified; the process of putting bands on birds.

barbs: on a feather, the parallel strands that branch off from the central stem.

barbules: the tiny, often hooked, strands along each barb of a feather.

behavior: actions. A bird's behaviors are the things it does.

breeding plumage: the feathers that cover a bird during the breeding season.

breeding range: the area where a particular kind of bird courts, mates, and rears its young.

brooder: A warm box that baby chicks are moved to after they hatch.

brooding: incubating eggs, or keeping chicks warm.

brood patch: a bare area on a bird's breast where the feathers have been removed to allow its body heat to warm its eggs or young.

brood parasite: a bird that does not build a nest or rear its own young, but lays its eggs in another bird's nest.

class: a group of related orders.

cloaca: the opening through which a bird's wastes, sperm, or eggs leave its body.

cockerels: adult, male chickens—also called roosters.

colony: a group of birds nesting near one another.

compete: to strive to obtain something, sometimes by challenging another. Birds may compete for nest sites, food, and other limited resources.

contour feathers: the outer layer of feathers on a bird's body that give it shape and enable it to fly.

coverts: the feathers that cover the bases of a bird's flight and tail feathers.

data: factual information.

depth perception: the ability to judge the distance of objects, and determine how far from one another different objects are.

display: a show of behavior.

distress call: a sound made by a bird when it is in trouble.

domesticated: raised by people.

down: small, fluffy feathers that form an insulating layer near the skin.

dominate: to control, or rule over others.

dust bathing: rolling in the dirt.

egg tooth: the small bump on a chick's beak used to break the eggshell when hatching.

embryo: an unhatched or unborn animal in an early stage of development.

evolve: to change gradually over time.

external ear: on some animals, a fleshy part of the ear that sticks out from the head.

family: a group of related genera (plural of genus).

fail: to be unsuccessful; in bird nests, to not produce healthy fledglings.

fecal sac: a membrane filled with wastes, produced by a young nestling.

fertile: able to produce young.

field of vision: the area visible through the eyes or through the lens of an instrument such as a telescope or pair of binoculars.

fledge: to leave the nest. Fledgeling birds still depend on their parents for care.

flock: a group of birds, usually of the same species.

gape: the soft tissue at the corners of a bird's beak.

genus: a group of related species.

hens: female chickens that have been laying eggs for over a year.

heronry: a colony of herons.

homeothermic: able to maintain a constant body temperature that is different from the surrounding air. "Warm-blooded."

humerus: the thigh-bone of a human or bird.

hybrids: the offspring of two birds (or other organisms) of different species.

incubate: to keep something warm so that it can develop.

incubator: a container used to keep eggs warm until they hatch.

inside and outside diameters: the inside diameter is the distance across the cup-shaped space inside the nest, and the outside diameter is the distance across the entire nest.

instinct: behavior that an animal displays without having learned it from any other animal.

interbreed: to mate and produce young with a member of a different species.

internal: inside the body.

kingdom: a group of living things. All animals belong to the kingdom *Animalia*.

membrane: a thin, soft layer of tissue that covers or lines a cell or organ.

migration: a regular, seasonal journey between wintering and breeding areas.

molting: replacing old, worn, feathers with new ones.

mounts: animals that appear life-like, although they have been preserved and stuffed.

nictating membrane: a transparent eyelid-like layer that moistens and cleans the eye.

obligatory parasite: a species that is unable to survive without parasitizing others.

order: a group of related families.

opportunistic: able to make use of whatever food or habitat is available.

ornithology: the study of birds.

parasites: organisms that live in or on other organisms. Parasites usually weaken or kill their hosts.

pecking order: in chickens, this term describes the ranking of birds in a flock. One bird is "boss," and others have various amounts of power.

pellets: packets of fur, bones, seeds, or other undigestible material that birds throw up after feeding.

pipping: to break open the shell of an egg when hatching.

precocial: young birds that are able to walk and look for food shortly after they hatch.

preening: in birds, the process of oiling and reorganizing the feathers with the beak.

primary feathers: the flight feathers along the trailing edge of a bird's wing, nearest the tip.

protective coloration: in birds, having feathers that blend in with the surroundings.

pullets: female chickens that have been laying eggs for a year or less.

race: a distinct group or breeding population within a species.

rachis: the stiff "stem" that runs down the middle of a feather.

radius: the smaller of two bones in the lower arm of a person, or the midde section of a bird's wing.

range maps: maps that show where particular birds can be found.

roost: a place where birds rest.

screamers: birds with slightly webbed feet that make up the family *Anhimidae*.

secondary feathers: flight feathers in the middle of the trailing edge of a bird's wing.

semiplumes: soft, fluffy feathers with a central "stem," or rachis.

shorebirds: wading birds, such as sandpipers and plovers, found along the coast.

silhouette: the outline or shape of the body of a bird or other animal.

social: relating to others. Social behavior involves interaction.

species: distinct kinds of organisms.

spring tides: the extra high (and extra low) tides that occur around the time of a full or new moon.

study skins: birds (or other animals) that have been preserved and stuffed. Study skins do not look particularly life-like.

suet: hard fat from sheep or cattle, often used to feed birds.

taxonomy: a system of classifying living creatures, such as birds, by grouping them according to shared physical characteristics.

tendons: tough cord-like tissue that connects muscles to bone.

territory: an area that an animal defends from others of its species, and uses to hunt or breed.

tertiary feathers: flight feathers along the trailing edge of a bird's wing, nearest the bird's body.

ulna: the larger of the two bones in the lower arm of a person or the middle section of a bird's wing.

uropygial gland: an oil gland located just above the tail in most birds.

vertebra: a bone in the back or neck of a bird or other animal.